Test-taker's Statement
for the TOEFL
Examination

A list of some important test-taking hints to review as you complete your preparation for the exam

1. *Read directions carefully.* Don't start out with a false assumption. Time is included to allow you to read the directions. Be sure you understand what is being asked.
2. *Consider all choices.* You must choose the *best* choice, not just a good choice.
3. *Avoid superstitions.* There is no pattern on a standardized test like the TOEFL. If you have just answered B four times in a row, the next answer has the same chance of being A, B, C, or D. Don't make choices for a problem based on answers from other problems.
4. *Mark your answer sheet clearly.* Use a soft lead pencil (No. 2) and blacken the choice completely. If you must erase an answer, erase it completely.
5. *Use your "Guess Answer."* Since no points are deducted for guessing, use answer (B) or (C) consistently when you have no idea which choice is correct.
6. *Concentrate.* Don't talk. Concentrate your attention. Don't look at anything in the test room except your test materials. Don't think about your score or your future. If you do, force your mind to return to the problem you are working on.
7. *Budget your time.* Calculate the time you may spend on each question so that you have enough time to

complete all of the questions on the test. Don't spend too much time on a question you can't answer.

8. *Check your answer sheet.* Be sure that you have marked your answer sheet completely.

9. *Don't cheat.* In spite of opportunity, knowledge that others are cheating, desire to help a friend, or fear that you will not make a good score, DON'T cheat. In the United States it is considered very serious. If you are discovered, your test materials will be taken, you will not be allowed to finish the examination, and your answer sheet will not be scored.

10. *Think positively.* Your attitude will influence your success on the TOEFL. Remember, you are not trying to score 100 percent. No one knows everything. If you have studied the material in this book and other books, you should feel prepared. Do your best!

BASIC TIPS

on the Test of English as a Foreign Language

TOEFL

Pamela J. Sharpe

Founding Director
American Language Institute
The University of Toledo

Barron's Educational Series, Inc.

Woodbury, New York • London • Toronto • Sydney

© Copyright 1982 by Barron's Educational Series, Inc.

All inquiries should be addressed to:
Barron's Educational Series, Inc.
113 Crossways Park Drive
Woodbury, New York 11797

Library of Congress Catalog Card No. 82-11649
International Standard Book No. 0-8120-2584-9

Library of Congress Cataloging in Publication Data

Sharpe, Pamela J.
  Basic tips on the TOEFL (Test of English as a foreign language)

  "Pocket-size edition of Barron's how to prepare for the TOEFL (Test of English as a foreign language)"—Pref.

  1. English language—Text-books for foreigners. 2. English language—Examinations, questions, etc. I. Barron's Educational Series, Inc. II. Title. III. Title: Basic tips on the T.O.E.F.L. (Test of English as a foreign language)
PE1128.A2S48 1982   428.2′4′076   82-11649
ISBN 0-8120-2584-9

PRINTED IN THE UNITED STATES OF AMERICA

2345 047 98765432

Contents

Preface

Seventy thousand students from 120 countries take the Test of English as a Foreign Language (TOEFL) every year at test centers in the United States and in their home countries. Some of them do not pass the TOEFL because they do not understand English. Others do not pass it because they do not understand the examination.

This book was designed to help you understand the TOEFL examination and prepare for it. It is a collection of practical suggestions along with two complete model tests.

It is a smaller, pocket-size edition of *Barron's How to Prepare for the TOEFL (Test of English as a Foreign Language)*.

Keep this convenient book handy for study on the bus, while you wait for appointments, or during breaks at work or school.

If you feel you need more review and practice, use the longer version of this book, *Barron's How to Prepare for the TOEFL (Test of English as a Foreign Language)* along with the companion workbook *Barron's Practice Exercises for the TOEFL and their accompanying cassettes*. In *Barron's How to Prepare for the TOEFL*, you will find review chapters for all three sections of the TOEFL— Listening Comprehension, Structure and Written Expression, Vocabulary and Reading Comprehension, as well as six model tests. In *Barron's Practice Exercises for the TOEFL*, you will find more than 1000 exercises for additional practice.

Study thoughtfully, and take the TOEFL with confidence. It may well be the most important examination of your academic career. And you can pass it.

Acknowledgments

The test instructions contained in this publication for the various sections of TOEFL have been reprinted with the permission of Educational Testing Service. The granting of this permission does not imply endorsement by ETS or the TOEFL program of the contents of this publication as a whole or of the practice questions that it contains. Since the types of questions in TOEFL and the instructions pertaining to them are subject to change, candidates who register to take TOEFL should read carefully the edition of the *TOEFL Bulletin* that will be sent to them free of charge with their admission tickets.

With the permission of Mr. Frank Berlen, excerpts have been selected and reprinted from the SEXTON TOEFL COURSE, a ten-week preparation program for TOEFL candidates offered by *Sexton Educational Programs,* New York City; Detroit, Michigan; Dallas, Texas.

Timetable for the TOEFL*
Total Time: 120 minutes

Section I (40 Minutes)	Listening Comprehension	50 Questions
Section II (25 Minutes)	Structure and Written Expression	40 Questions
Section III (55 Minutes)	Reading Comprehension and Vocabulary	60 Questions

* Note: Actual times will vary in accordance with the time the proctor completes the preliminary work and begins the actual test. Format and timing subject to change.

1

Questions and Answers Concerning the New TOEFL

The following questions are commonly asked by students as they prepare for the Test of English as a Foreign Language (TOEFL). To help you, they have been answered here.

What Is The Purpose Of The TOEFL?

Since 1963 the TOEFL has been used by scholarship selection committees of governments, universities, and agencies such as Fulbright, the Agency for International Development, AMID EAST, Latin American Scholarship Program and others as a standard measure of the English proficiency of their candidates.

The majority of admissions committees of colleges and universities in the United States require foreign applicants to submit TOEFL scores along with transcripts and recommendations in order to be considered for admission. Some colleges and universities in Canada and other English-speaking countries also require the TOEFL for admissions purposes.

Many universities use TOEFL scores to fulfill the foreign language requirement for doctoral candidates whose first language is not English.

What Is An International TOEFL Testing?

The TOEFL is offered six times a year on regularly scheduled Saturdays in August, October, November, January, March, and May at designated test centers in 135 countries throughout the world, including all of the states of the United States. This is called an International TOEFL Testing. A list of test centers established for the purpose of administering the International TOEFL Testing appears in the free *TOEFL Bulletin of Information and Application Form* available from the TOEFL Office.

In order to receive a copy of the *TOEFL Bulletin of Information and Application Form* write:

> TOEFL Office
> Box 899
> Princeton, New Jersey
> 08451 U.S.A.

It is correct to limit your letter to two sentences. For example:

A Letter of Request for the *TOEFL Bulletin of Information and Application Form*

> (write your address here)
> (write the date here)

TOEFL Office
Box 899
Princeton, New Jersey
08451 U.S.A.

Dear Sir:

Please send a copy of the TOEFL Bulletin of Information and Application Form to the address above.

Thank you for your earliest attention.

> Sincerely yours,
> (write your name here)

The TOEFL Bulletin is also available overseas in U.S. embassies and offices of the United States International Communication Agency (binational centers) as well as IIE and AMID EAST Counseling Centers.

What Is An Institutional TOEFL Testing?

Some language institutes affiliated with schools and universities in the United States and abroad adjust their test dates to correspond to the university calendar. Test dates are usually in March, June, August, and December. This is called an Institutional TOEFL Testing. It is generally offered to the students who have just finished an intensive English course in the institute administering the TOEFL.

If you plan to take the TOEFL at an Institutional TOEFL Testing, confirm your eligibility with the director of the institute at least one month in advance of the test date. The examination will probably be given on the campus of the school or university with which the language institute is affiliated.

What Is A Special Center Testing?

There are more than eighty Special TOEFL Test Centers located in fifty countries where tests are offered six times a year on regularly scheduled Fridays.

A list of Special TOEFL Test Centers appears in the free *TOEFL Bulletin of Information and Application Form*.

Which Language Skills Are Tested On The TOEFL?

Prior to September, 1976, five language skills were tested in five separate sections:

Language Skills Tested Prior to September, 1976

Section I	Listening Comprehension
Section II	English Structure
Section III	Vocabulary
Section IV	Reading Comprehension
Section V	Writing Ability

There were 200 questions tested.

The same five language skills are tested in the New TOEFL. They are tested in three sections:

Language Skills Tested in the New TOEFL

Section I	Listening Comprehension
Section II	Structure and Written Expression
Section III	Reading Comprehension and Vocabulary

There are 150 questions tested.

Are Scores Considered The Same For All Testings?

There is no difference in the scores from an International TOEFL Testing, an Institutional TOEFL Testing, or a Special TOEFL Center Testing.

However, if you plan to send your scores to several colleges or universities for admissions purposes, you should take the International or Special Center Test. The scores from an Institutional Test can be used only by the institution where you take the test.

Is The New TOEFL Used For All Testings?

The New TOEFL is now used for all International Testings, Institutional Testings, and Special Center Testings in the United States and around the world.

How Do I Register For An International Testing?

An application form is included in the free *TOEFL Bulletin of Information and Application Form.*

If you are living in the United States, return the application along with a $19 registration fee to TOEFL Office, Box 899, Princeton, New Jersey 08541.

If you are living in another country, return the application along with a $19 registration fee to the TOEFL agent for your country. TOEFL agents are listed in the *TOEFL Bulletin of Information.* If your country does not have a TOEFL agent, return the application and fee to TOEFL, Box 899–R, Princeton, New Jersey 08541. U.S.A.

All fees must be paid in U.S. dollars. Pay by check, bank draft, or money order.

If you are living in a country where it is difficult to comply with this regulation, mail your completed application to a friend or relative living in the United States, Canada, or a country where checks, bank drafts, or money orders may be drawn on banks in the United States. Your friend or relative may mail the application and fee directly to the TOEFL office.

The check, bank draft, or money order must be made out to TOEFL and your TOEFL application number must appear on it.

How Do I Register For An Institutional Testing?

You will need to fill out the same application form that is used in an International Testing, but it will probably not be necessary for you to write to the TOEFL Office in order to secure one. The language institute that administers the Institutional Testing should have application forms available. Fees vary from $10 to $19.

The institute will return your application form and the registration fee to the TOEFL Office along with the forms and fees of all of the other applicants for the Institutional Testing. You will receive your Confirmation Ticket from the language institute.

How Do I Register For A Special Center Testing?

Registration for a Special Center Testing is the same as for an International Testing.

The fee for a Special Center Testing is $27.

Will Educational Testing Service Confirm My Registration?

One month before your test date, the TOEFL Office will mail you a registration Confirmation Ticket and a copy of the *Handbook for Examinees*. Read the handbook carefully and follow the instructions.

May I Change The Date Or Cancel My Registration?

Test date changes are not permitted. If you want to take the test on another date, you must send in a new application form with another check or money order for $19.

If you do not take the test, you can send your confirmation ticket to the TOEFL Office in Princeton, New Jersey. If they receive your request within sixty days of your test date, you will receive part of your money as a refund.

May I Register On The Day Of The TOEFL Examination?

Registration of candidates on the day of the TOEFL examination is not permitted under any circumstances at test centers in the United States. At test centers outside of the United States, candidates may register on the day of the examination only if space and materials are available and if the candidate presents positive identification along with a letter of request signed by a representative of the United States Embassy, A.I.D., or a sponsoring agency or university.

What Should I Take With Me To The Examination Room?

Take three sharpened number-two pencils with erasers on them, your Confirmation Ticket, and photo identification. It would be very helpful to take a watch. Books, dictionaries, tape recorders, and notes are not permitted in the examination room.

Where Should I Sit?

If you have an opportunity to choose your seat, try to locate the speakers attached to the tape recorder or record player which will be used in the Listening Comprehension Section of the examination. Even though the tape recorder or record player is in the front of the room, the speakers may be set up in the back of the room. Choose a seat near the speakers, but not directly in front of them.

If you do not have an opportunity to choose a seat, don't worry. It is the responsibility of the examiner to assure that everyone is able to hear the tape or record. If you can't hear well, ask the examiner to adjust the volume.

How Long Is The Testing Session Of The New TOEFL?

The total time for the testing session of the new TOEFL is 120 minutes. Since the instructions are not included as part of the timed sections, the actual time which you will spend in the examination room will be a little longer than 120 minutes.

How Much Time Do I Have To Complete Each Of The Sections?

It is wise to work as rapidly as possible without compromising accuracy. Check the Timetable for the TOEFL on page ix and read the suggestions for working more rapidly included on the beginning pages of this edition.

How Do I Answer The Test Questions?

Read the four possible answers in your test book and mark the corresponding space on the answer sheet which will be provided for you at the test center.

We have included typical answer sheets with the model examinations included in this book. Because it takes a little longer to finish an examination when you mark the answers on a separate sheet, use the answer sheets when you take the timed model examinations in this book.

How Do I Mark The Answer Sheet?

Before the examination begins, the examiner will explain how to mark the answer sheet. Be sure to fill in the space completely.

One question is shown in the test book. One answer is marked on the answer sheet.

1. The United States is a country in
    (A) South America
    (B) Central America
    (C) North America
    (D) Antarctica

1. Ⓐ   Ⓑ   ●   Ⓓ

May I Erase An Answer?

You may erase an answer if you do so carefully and completely. Stray pencil marks may cause inaccurate scoring by the test-scoring machine.

If I Am Not Sure Of An Answer, Should I Guess?

If you are not sure of an answer, you should guess. The number of incorrect answers is not subtracted from your score. Your score is based upon the number of correct answers only.

Do not mark more than one answer for each question. Do not leave any questions blank on your answer sheet.

How Should I Guess?

First, eliminate all of the possibilities which you know are not correct. Then, if you are almost sure of an answer, guess that one.

If you have no idea of the correct answer for a question, choose one letter and use it for your "guess" answer throughout the entire examination.

By using the same letter each time that you guess, you will probably answer correctly 25 percent of the time. This percentage is usually better than the percentage of correct answers obtained by random guessing.

The "guess" answer is especially useful for finishing a section quickly. If the examiner tells you to stop working on a section before you have finished it, answer all of the remaining questions with the "guess" answer.

What Should I Do If I Discover That I Have Marked My Answer Sheet Incorrectly?

Do not panic. Notify the examiner immediately.

If you have marked one answer in the wrong space on the answer sheet, the rest of the answers will be out of sequence. Ask for time at the end of the examination to correct the sequence.

If you have marked the answers in the test book instead of on the answer sheet, ask for your test book to be attached to your answer sheet and included in the examiner's "Irregularities Report."

In order to avoid mismarking and to save space on your desk, use your test book as a marker on your answer sheet. As you advance, slide the book down underneath the number of the question which you are marking on the answer sheet.

If I Score Very Poorly On One Part Of The Examination, Is It Still Possible To Receive A Good Total Score?

If you have mismarked an entire part of a section, or if you feel that you have done very poorly on one part of a section, do not despair. You may receive a low score on one part of a section and still score well on the total examination if your scores on the other parts of that section and the other sections are good.

How Is My TOEFL Test Scored?

First, each of the three sections of the TOEFL is graded on a scale from 20 to 80. Then the scores from the three sections are added together. Finally, the sum is multiplied by 3⅓.

For example, the following scores were received on the three sections.

Listening Comprehension	52
Structure and Written Expression	48
Reading Comprehension and Vocabulary	50
	150

150 × 3⅓ = 500 Total TOEFL Score

How Do I Interpret My Score?

There are no passing or failing scores on the TOEFL. Each agency or university will evaluate the scores according to its own requirements. Even at the same university, the requirements may vary for different programs of study.

The admissions policies summarized below are typical of American universities, assuming of course, that the applicant's documents other than English proficiency are acceptable.

Typical Admissions Policies of American Universities

TOEFL Score	Policy
550 or more	admission assured
500–549	admission probable
450–499	individual cases reviewed
449 or less	admission doubtful to university; admission possible to two-year college

Refer to the *Handbook for Examinees* for a detailed chart of percentile ranks for total TOEFL scores. This will help you interpret your score relative to the scores of others taking the examination.

When Will I Receive My Score Report?

You are entitled to five copies of your test results, including an Examinee's Score Confirmation Record for yourself and four Official Score Reports.

You will receive your Examinee's Score Confirmation Record about one month after you take the test.

How Will The Agencies Or Universities Of My Choice Be Informed Of My Score?

One month after the testing, your Official Score Reports will be forwarded directly to the agencies and/or universities which you designated on an Information Section at the top of the TOEFL answer sheet on the day of the examination.

If you have marked fewer than four institutions or agencies on your answer sheet, the extra copies of your test results will be sent to you with your Examinee's Score Confirmation Forms.

You may send the copies to an institution or agency, but the score will probably have to be confirmed by an official at the TOEFL Office before you can be admitted.

May I Take The TOEFL More Than One Time?

You may take the TOEFL as many times as you wish in order to score to your satisfaction.

If I Have Already Taken The TOEFL, How Will The First Score Or Scores Affect My New Score?

TOEFL scores are considered to be valid for two years. If you have taken the TOEFL more than once, but your first score report is dated more than two years ago, the TOEFL Office will not report your score.

If you have taken the TOEFL more than once in the past two years, your highest score will usually be considered.

How Difficult Is The TOEFL?

The level of difficulty of the TOEFL is directly related to the average level of proficiency in English of the candidates who take the examination.

This means that each question will probably be answered correctly by 50 percent of the candidates.

Is There A Direct Correspondence Between Proficiency In English And A Good Score On The TOEFL?

There is not always a direct correspondence between proficiency in English and a good score on the TOEFL. Many students who are proficient in English are not proficient in how to approach the examination. That is why it is important to prepare by using this book.

2

Basic Tips for Section I: Listening Comprehension

Part A   Statements

BASIC TIP 1   **Teens and tens**

> *Teens* are numbers like thirteen, fourteen, fifteen, sixteen, seventeen, eighteen, and nineteen. *Tens* are numbers like thirty, forty, fifty, sixty, seventy, eighty, and ninety.
>
> In some statements on Part A, you will have to hear the difference between a teen and a ten in order to answer problems correctly.
>
> When you hear a statement, you must decide whether the number is a teen or ten. For example, thirteen or thirty.

EXAMPLE:
   Statement: Take the number seventeen bus to the shopping center and transfer to the ten.
   Restatement: The 17 bus goes to the shopping center.

BASIC TIP 2   Computations

Computations means simple mathematics.

In some statements on Part A, you will have to add, subtract, multiply, or divide in order to answer the problems correctly. In other statements, you will be given all of the information and you will NOT need to add, etc.

When you hear a statement, you must decide whether it is necessary to compute the answer. If you need to make a computation, you must be accurate.

EXAMPLE:
Statement: I thought that I had set the alarm clock for seven o'clock, but it rang an hour early.

Restatement: The alarm rang at six o'clock.

BASIC TIP 3   Minimal pairs

Minimal pairs are words that sound almost alike.

In some statements on Part A, you will hear a word that sounds almost like another word.

When you hear a statement, you must listen carefully to the sounds.

EXAMPLE:
Statement: I thought her last name was "Best," but it was "Past."

Restatement: She is Mrs. Past (not Best).

BASIC TIP 4 Synonyms

> *Synonyms* are words that have the same meaning.
>
> In some statements on Part A, you will hear a word that has a common synonym.
>
> When you hear a statement, you must know the meaning of the words. You must be able to recognize a synonym.

EXAMPLE:

Statement: My roommate always prepares dinner for us.

Restatement: My roommate fixes our dinner.

BASIC TIP 5 Negatives

> *Negatives* are negations of affirmative statements.
>
> In some statements on Part A, you will hear a negative or a double negative.
>
> When you hear a negative or a double negative, you must be able to restate the information.

EXAMPLE:

Statement: Not one student has bought enough insurance.

Restatement: None of the students is sufficiently insured.

BASIC TIP 6   **References**

Reference means the person referred to in a statement.

In some statements on Part A, you will hear two or three names.

When you hear a statement, you must remember how each person was referred to.

EXAMPLE:
Statement: Tom doesn't know whether his father will allow his sister to come to the United States to study.
Restatement: Tom's sister may come to the United States.

BASIC TIP 7   **Comparatives**

Comparatives are comparisons of two or more people or things. In many ways, Comparatives are like References.

In some statements on Part A, you will hear descriptions of two or three people or things.

When you hear a statement, you must remember how each was compared with the other.

EXAMPLE:
Statement: Mary gets better grades in English than she does in math.
Restatement: Mary's grades in math are not as good as her grades in English.

BASIC TIP 8   Conditionals

Conditionals are statements of conditions and imagined re-sults.

In some statements on Part A, you will hear a conditional introduced by the word *if*; in others, you will hear a conditional introduced by the word *whether* or *unless*.

When you hear a statement, you must be able to restate the information as facts instead of imagined results.

EXAMPLE:

Statement: We would have had a good time at the football game if it hadn't been so cold.

Restatement: We didn't have a good time because it was too cold.

BASIC TIP 9   Concessions

Concessions are statements of unexpected results.

In some statements on Part A, you will hear a concession introduced by the word *but*. The word *instead* or *anyway* may be the last word in the statement.

When you hear a statement, you must be able to restate the information.

EXAMPLE:

Statement: The computer will be available any time but one o'clock.

Restatement: The computer will not be available at one o'clock.

BASIC TIP 10   More Concessions

Remember, *Concessions* are statements of unexpected results.

In some statements on Part A, you will hear a Concession introduced by a situation with *although, though, even though, in spite of, despite,* or *contrary to.*

When you hear a statement, you must be able to restate the information.

EXAMPLE:

Statement: Contrary to what Ellen had expected, the city was very nice.

Restatement: Ellen had not expected the city to be nice.

BASIC TIP 11   Causals

Causals are statements of cause or explanation.

In some statements on Part A, you will hear a causal introduced by the word *since* or *because.*

When you hear a statement, you must be able to restate the information.

EXAMPLE:

Statement: Since Mark couldn't find his key he had to pay for it.

Restatement: Mark paid for his key because he lost it.

BASIC TIP 12   Cause and effect adjectives

Cause and effect adjectives are adjectives that end in *-ing* or *-ed*. They are usually verbals from verbs such as *surprise*, *interest*, *bore*, *encourage*, and *annoy*.

In some statements on Part A, you will hear a cause adjective, an effect adjective, or a verb form.

When you hear a statement, you must be able to restate the information.

EXAMPLE:

Statement: The project interests my professor.
Restatement: My professor is interested in the project.

BASIC TIP 13   Chronological events

Chronological events are events that take place in time relationship to each other.

In some statements on Part A, two or more events will be mentioned.

When you hear a statement, you must remember which event took place first, second, and so on.

EXAMPLE:

Statement: We plan to meet at the car a few minutes after the shopping center closes.
Restatement: The shopping center will close before we meet at the car.

Part B   Conversations

BASIC TIP 14   **Direct conversations**

Direct means stated.

In some conversations on Part B, you will hear all of the information that you need to answer the problem correctly. You will NOT need to draw conclusions.

When you hear a conversation between two speakers, you must remember the details that were stated.

EXAMPLE:

Man:	Tell me about your trip to New York.
Woman:	It was great! We saw the Statue of Liberty and the Empire State Building and all of the tourist attractions the first day, then we saw the museums the second day, and spent the rest of the time shopping and seeing shows.
Third Voice:	What are the man and woman talking about?
Answer:	The woman's trip.

BASIC TIP 15   Computation conversations

Remember, *Computations* means simple mathematics.

In some conversations on Part B, you will have to add, subtract, multiply, or divide in order to answer the problems correctly. In other conversations, you will be given all of the information, and you will NOT need to add, etc.

When you hear a conversation between two speakers, you must decide whether it is necessary to compute the answer to the question asked by the third voice. If you need to make a computation, you must be accurate.

EXAMPLE:

Woman: How many stamps do I need to send this package airmail?

Man: Airmail? Well, that's going to be expensive. Airmail postage is 32 cents for the first ounce and 24 cents for each additional ounce. You have eleven ounces here.

Third Voice: How much will it cost the woman to mail her package?

Answer: $2.72.

BASIC TIP 16   Place conversations

Place means the location where the conversation occurred.

In some conversations on Part B, you will hear words and phrases that will suggest a location. For example, "books," a "card catalog," and a "check-out desk" suggest a "library."

When you hear a conversation between two speakers, you must listen for information that will help you draw a conclusion about where the conversation most probably took place.

EXAMPLE:

Woman:	I'll need a dozen three-penny nails and six wood screws, too.
Man:	The screws come in packages of ten for ninety-nine cents. I hope that's all right.
Third Voice:	Where does this conversation most probably take place?
Answer:	At the hardware store.

BASIC TIP 17   Implied conversations

Implied means suggested, but not stated. In many ways, Implied conversations are like Place conversations.

In some conversations on Part B, you will hear words and phrases or intonations that will suggest how the speakers felt, what they will probably do, or what kind of work or activity that they were involved in during the conversation.

When you hear a conversation between two speakers, you must listen for information that will help you draw a conclusion about the situation.

EXAMPLE:

Man: Could you please book me on the next flight out to Los Angeles?

Woman: I'm sorry, sir. Continental doesn't fly into Los Angeles. Why don't you try Delta or Trans World?

Third Voice: What will the man probably do?

Answer: He will probably get a ticket for a flight on Delta or Trans World Airlines.

Part C   Mini Talks

Note: The examples in the following Basic Tips are shorter than the actual mini talks on the TOEFL examination. The actual mini talks usually have four questions following them.

Longer mini talks with four questions are printed in *Barron's How to Prepare for the TOEFL (Test of English as a Foreign Language)*.

BASIC TIP 18   Overheard conversations

Overheard conversations are conversations heard by someone who is not talking.

In some talks on Part C, you will hear a long conversation between two or three speakers.

When you hear a conversation, you must be able to summarize the important ideas. You will usually NOT be required to remember small details.

EXAMPLE:

Ted Parker:	Are you Mrs. Williams?
Mrs. Williams:	Why yes.
Ted Parker:	I'm Ted Parker. I talked with you on the telephone earlier today.
Mrs. Williams:	Oh, good.
Ted Parker:	Let me show you what we have in a new Oldsmobile Cutlass.
Mrs. Williams:	I want to look at last year's model, too, if you have any.
Ted Parker:	I have one. A red Delta 88 with 2,000 miles on it. It was a demonstrator.

Mrs. Williams: A demonstrator?
Ted Parker: That means that only the sales staff have driven it.

Question: Who is the man?
Answer: A car salesman.

BASIC TIP 19   Announcements and advertisements

Announcements are short talks that provide factual information. *Advertisements* are short talks that provide persuasive information.

In some talks on Part C, you will hear factual or persuasive information.

When you hear a talk, you must be able to summarize the important ideas. You must also be able to answer questions that begin with the following words: *who, what, when, why?*

EXAMPLE:

During this holiday season you'll be glad that you took pictures. So get kodacolor film at Foto-land, this week only, two rolls for $3.25. Remember, good pictures start with good film, and kodacolor is the best!

Get your film now at Foto-land and bring it back after the holiday to be developed. Unless we develop your pictures in three days, you don't pay us a penny, and you never pay unless they turn out like you want them to.

With Foto-land, you can depend on larger, clearer prints. Pictures will make your memories of this Christmas last forever.

From all of us at Foto-land, best wishes for a Merry Christmas, and many more pictures this year!

Question: What is the advertisement about?
Answer: Film and film processing.

BASIC TIP 20   News reports

News Reports are short talks that provide information about the news of the day.

In some talks on Part C, you will hear information about the news.

When you hear a talk, you must be able to summarize the information. You will usually NOT be required to remember small details.

EXAMPLE:

Today's story is about the flight from the cities. Everyone knows that it is happening, but only recently have we been able to determine where people are going. To the suburbs? To the fringes of the city? Surprisingly not. In a marked reversal of U.S. migration patterns non-metropolitan areas have started growing faster than metropolitan areas. City dwellers are leaving to settle in small-town America.

New census figures confirm both the shrinkage of many urban areas and the revival of small towns, a trend that began to become apparent in the last decade. While the national population increased by 4.8 percent from 1970–1975, towns of 2,500–25,000 persons rose 7.5 percent, and the smallest towns with populations of less than 2,500 rose 8.7 percent, or nearly double the national rate.

Question: What is the topic of this talk?
Answer: Migration out of the cities.

BASIC TIP 21   Weather reports

Weather reports are short talks that predict the weather.

In some talks on Part C, you will hear predictions of the weather.

When you hear a talk, you must be able to summarize the prediction. You will usually NOT be required to remember small details.

EXAMPLE:

Good morning. This is Danny Jackson with the Weather Watch, brought to you every day at this time by the Austin Chamber of Commerce. The week-long extended forecast for Austin and the Texas Hill Country calls for mostly sunny weather today and Tuesday with temperatures in the high seventies. By Wednesday, a cold pressure area that has been building out over the Gulf of Mexico should begin to move inland over Texas bringing about a ten-degree drop in temperatures over the south central part of the state. By Wednesday night that same low pressure should probably be dropping rain over the Austin area, with rain continuing into Thursday and possibly even early Friday. By Friday afternoon though, if all goes well, we should begin to see clear skies again with a corresponding rise in temperatures back into the seventies. Saturday and Sunday look like they'll be just beautiful. Danny Jackson with Weather Watch. Have a good week, Austin.

Question: What is the weather forecast for the week?
Answer: Sunny today with rain toward the middle of the week and sunshine again on the weekend.

BASIC TIP 22 Informative speeches

Informative speeches are short talks that provide factual information. In many ways, Informative speeches are like Announcements and Advertisements.

In some talks on Part C, you will hear factual information.

When you hear a talk, you must be able to summarize the important ideas. You must also be able to answer questions that begin with the following words: *who, what, when, where, why?*

EXAMPLE:

Welcome to the Lincoln Memorial, located, as you can see, on the west bank of the Potomac River on the axis of the Capitol Building and the Washington Monument.

The structure itself was designed by Henry Bacon in 1912, and completed ten years later at a cost of 2.9 million dollars.

The outer walls of the memorial are white Colorado marble, 189 feet long and 118 feet, 8 inches wide. The thirty-six outer columns are also of marble, representing the thirty-six states that were in the Union at the time of Lincoln's death. The name of each state is cut into stone above the column.

Inside the memorial, the walls are Indiana limestone and the floor is pink Tennessee marble. Three commemorative features include the huge seated statue of Lincoln and two inscribed stone tablets.

Question: Why are there thirty-six columns?
Answer: There is one for each state in the Union at the time of Lincoln's death.

BASIC TIP. 23   Academic statements

Academic statements are short talks that provide academic information. They are like short lectures that might be heard in a college classroom.

In some talks on Part C, you will hear academic information.

When you hear a talk, you must be able to summarize the important ideas. You must also be able to answer questions that begin with the following words: *who, what, when, where, why?*

EXAMPLE:

Ernest Hemingway began his writing career as an ambitious, young American newspaperman in Paris after the First World War. His early books, including *The Sun Also Rises*, were published in Europe before they were released in the United States.

Hemingway always wrote from experience rather than from imagination. In *Farewell to Arms*, published in 1929, he recounted his adventures as an ambulance driver in Italy during the war. In *For Whom the Bell Tolls*, published in 1940, he retold his memories of the Spanish Civil War.

Perhaps more than any other twentieth-century American writer, he was responsible for creating a style of literature. The Hemingway style was hard, economical, and powerful. It lured the reader into using imagination in order to fill in the details.

In 1952, Hemingway published *The Old Man and the Sea*, a short, compelling tale of an old fisherman's struggle to haul in a giant marlin that he had caught in the Gulf of Mexico. Some critics interpreted it as the allegory of man's struggle against old age; others interpreted it as man against the forces of nature. The climax of Hemingway's career, the book was awarded the Nobel Prize for literature in 1954.

Question: Which book won the Nobel Prize for literature?

Answer: The Old Man and the Sea.

BASIC TIP 24   Class discussions

Class discussions are conversations that occur in classrooms. Class discussions are like Overheard conversations.

In some talks on Part C, you will hear a long conversation between two, three, or more speakers.

When you hear a conversation, you must be able to summarize the important ideas. You will usually NOT be required to remember small details.

EXAMPLE:

Miss Richards: Good morning. My name is Miss Richards and I'll be your instructor for Career Education 100. Before we get started I'd appreciate it if you would introduce yourselves, and tell us a little bit about why you decided to take this class. let's start here . . .

Bill: I'm Bill Jensen, and I'm a sophomore this term, but I still haven't decided what to major in. I hope that this class will help me.

Miss Richards: Good, I hope so, too. Next.

Patty: I'm Patty Davis and I'm majoring in foreign languages, but I'm not sure what kind of job I can get after I graduate.

Miss Richards:	Are you a sophomore too, Patty?
Patty:	No. I'm a senior. I wish I'd taken this class sooner but I didn't know about it until this term.
Question:	What are the man and woman talking about?
Answer:	They are introducing themselves.

3

Basic Tips for Section II: Structure and Written Expression

Part A Structure

BASIC TIP 25 **Verbs that require an infinitive or an *-ing* form in the complement**

S	V	C	M
We	had planned	to leave	day before yesterday

Remember that the following verbs require an infinitive in the complement:

agree	intend
decide	learn
expect	plan
fail	promise
hope	refuse
	want

Avoid using an *-ing* form after the verbs listed. Avoid using a verb word after *want*.

S	V	C	M
He	enjoys	traveling	by plane

Remember that the following verbs require an *-ing* form in the complement:

admit	deny	quit
appreciate	enjoy	regret
avoid	finish	risk
consider	practice	stop

Avoid using an infinitive after the verbs listed.

Forbid may be used with either an infinitive or an *-ing* complement, but *forbid from* is not idiomatic.

S	V Ph	C	M
She	forgot about	canceling	her appointment

Remember that the following verb phrases require an *-ing* form in the complement:

approve of	do not mind	keep on
be better off	forget about	look forward to
can't help	get through	object to
count on	insist on	think about
		think of

Avoid using an infinitive after the verb phrases listed. Avoid using a verb word after *look forward to* and *object to*.

EXAMPLE:
  Incorrect: She is considering not to go.
  Correct: She is considering not *going*.

BASIC TIP 26   Participles

HAVE participle
The concert had   begun before we could find our seats
Remember that the participles of the following verbs are not the same as the past forms.
Avoid using a past form instead of a participle with *have, has, had,* or *having.*

Verb Word	Past Form	Participle
begin	*began*	*begun*
come	*came*	*come*
choose	*chose*	*chosen*
drink	*drank*	*drunk*
fall	*fell*	*fallen*
give	*gave*	*given*
know	*knew*	*known*
run	*ran*	*run*
see	*saw*	*seen*
speak	*spoke*	*spoken*
steal	*stole*	*stolen*
take	*took*	*taken*
tear	*tore*	*torn*
go	*went*	*gone*
wear	*wore*	*worn*
write	*wrote*	*written*

EXAMPLE:

Incorrect: Someone had broken into the office and stole the files.

Correct: Someone *had* broken into the office and *stolen* the files.

BASIC TIP 27　　　**Necessity, usually for repair or improvement**

S	NEED	-*ing* form
This paragraph	needs	revising
Avoid using an infinitive or a participle instead of an -*ing* form.		

or

S	NEED	to be	participle
This paragraph	needs	to be	revised
Avoid using an -*ing* form instead of a participle.			

EXAMPLE:
Incorrect: His car needs to fix.
Correct:　His car needs *fixing*.
　　　　　　　　or
　　　　　　His car needs *to be fixed*.

BASIC TIP 28　　　**Ability**

S	KNOW	noun
I	know	the answer
Avoid using an infinitive after *know*.		

S	KNOW	how	infinitive	
I	know	how	to answer	the question
Remember that *how* must be used with an infinitive.				

EXAMPLE:

Incorrect: If she knew to drive, he would lend her his car.

Correct: If she *knew how to drive*, he would lend her his car.

BASIC TIP 29   Past custom

S	used to	verb word	
He	used to	live	in the country

Avoid using a form of *be* after the subject. Avoid using the incorrect form *use to*.

S	BE	used to	*-ing* form	
He	was	used to	living	in the country

Avoid using a form of *be* after *used to*. Avoid using a verb word instead of an *-ing* form. Avoid using the incorrect form *use to*.

EXAMPLE:

Incorrect: I used to was studying at the University of Southern California before I transferred here.

Correct: I *used to study* at the University of Southern California before I transferred here.

or

I *was used to studying* at the University of Southern California before I transferred here.

BASIC TIP 30   Logical conclusions

S	must have	participle	past time
My friend	must have	called	last night
S	**must be**	***-ing***	**present time**
My friend	must be	calling	now
S	**must**	**verb word**	**repeated time**
My friend	must	call	often

Remember that an observation in the present may serve as the basis for a conclusion about something that happened in the past. For example, "here is a message on my desk." It may be concluded that "my friend must have called last night."

Avoid using *should* or *can* instead of *must*. Avoid using a verb word instead of *have* and a participle when referring to a past occurrence.

EXAMPLE:
  Incorrect: The streets are wet; it should have rained last night.
  Correct: The streets are wet; it *must have rained* last night.

BASIC TIP 31   Advisability

S   had better verb word
You had better   take   Chemistry 600 this semester
S   had better not verb word
You had better not   take   Chemistry 600 this semester
Remember that although *had* is a past form, it refers to future time in this pattern. Avoid using an infinitive or a past form of a verb instead of a verb word. Avoid using *don't* instead of *not*.

EXAMPLE:
  Incorrect: You had better to hurry if you don't want to miss the bus.
  Correct: You *had better hurry* if you want to miss the bus.

BASIC TIP 32   **Question forms for invitations and customs**

Would you like	**infinitive**	
Would you like	to watch	the news today?

Remember that *would like* means to want. It is used in a question form for an invitation. A specific date such as *today* is usually included.

Avoid using *will* and *won't* instead of *would*. Avoid using *do* instead of *would* for invitations.

Do you like	**infinitive**	
Do you like	to watch	the news every day?

Remember that *like* means to enjoy. It is used with *do* in a question form for asking about customs. A word or phrase indicating habitual action such as *every day* is usually included.

Avoid using *would* instead of *do* for customs.

EXAMPLE:

Incorrect: Do you like to come to a party on Saturday at the International House?

Correct: *Would you like* to come to a party *on Saturday* at the International House?

BASIC TIP 33   Preference

S	would rather		verb word		
I	would rather		drive		
S	would rather	not	verb word		
I	would rather	not	drive		
Avoid using an infinitive or an *-ing* form instead of a verb word.					
S	would rather	that	S	V (past)	
I	would rather	that	you	drove	
Avoid using a present verb or a verb word instead of a past verb. Avoid using *should* and a verb word instead of a past verb.					
S	would rather	that	S	didn't	verb word
I	would rather	that	you	didn't	drive
Avoid using *don't* or *doesn't* instead of *didn't*.					

EXAMPLE:
  Incorrect: I'd rather that you don't do that.
  Correct: I'd *rather that you didn't do* that.

BASIC TIP 34   **Unfulfilled desires in the past**

S	had hoped	that	S	would	verb word	
We	had hoped	that	she	would	change	her mind

Avoid using a verb word instead of *would* and a verb word.
Avoid using the incorrect pattern:

S	had hoped	object pronoun	*-ing* form	
We	had hoped	her	changing	her mind

EXAMPLE:

Incorrect: He had hoped that he graduate this semester, but he couldn't finish his thesis in time.

Correct: He had hoped *that he would graduate* this semester, but he couldn't finish his thesis in time.

BASIC TIP 35　　　Conditions

If　S　V (present)　　　　　　　　, S　will　verb word
If　we　find　her address, we　will　write　her
or
S　will　verb word　if　S　V (present)
We　will　write　her if we　find　her address
Avoid using a present verb instead of *will* and a verb word.
If　S　V̂ (past)　　　　　　　, S　would　verb word
If　we　found　her address, we　would　write　her
or
S　would　verb word　if　S　V (past)
We　would　write　her if we　found　her address
Avoid using *would* and a verb word instead of a past verb.

If	S	had	participle		,	S	would have could have	participle
If	we	had	found	her address,	we		would have	written	her
If	we	had	found	her address,	we		could have	written	her

or

	S	would have could have	participle	if	S	had	participle
We		would have	written	her if	we	had	found	her address
We		could have	written	her if	we	had	found	her address

Avoid using *would have* and a participle instead of *had* and a participle. Avoid using *have* as a participle.

EXAMPLE:

Incorrect: If you listen to the questions carefully, you answer them easily.

Correct: *If you listen* to the questions carefully, *you will answer* them easily.

or

You will answer them easily *if you listen* to the questions carefully.

BASIC TIP 36 **Desires**

| | | | had
could have | |
| | | | would have participle | |
S WISH (present)		that S		
I	wish	that you	had	called	yesterday
I	wish	that you	could have	called	yesterday
I	wish	that you	would have	called	yesterday

Remember that although the verb *WISH* is in present tense, this pattern refers to desires in the past.

| | | | V (past)
could verb word
would verb word | |
S WISH (present)		that S		
I	wish	that you	called	every day
I	wish	that you	could call	tomorrow
I	wish	that you	would call	tomorrow

Remember that although the verb *WISH* is in present tense, this pattern refers to desires for customs and future events.

Avoid using this pattern to express desires in the past. Avoid using *will* instead of *could* and *would*.

EXAMPLE:

Incorrect: I wish that I received this letter before the office closed for the day.

Correct: I wish that I *had received* this letter before the office closed for the day.

or

I wish that I *could have received* this letter before the office closed for the day.

or

I wish that I *would have received* this letter before the office closed for the day.

BASIC TIP 37   Contrary-to-fact statements

If	S	were	
If	the party	were	on Friday, we could go

Avoid changing *were* to agree with the subject in contrary-to-fact statements.

S	WISH (present)	that	S	were	
I	wish	that	the party	were	on Friday

Avoid changing *were* to agree with the subject.

EXAMPLE:

Incorrect: If I was you, I would not go.

Correct: If I *were* you, I would not go.

BASIC TIP 38   Subjunctives

S	V	that	S	verb word	
Mr. Johnson	prefers	that	she	speak	with him personally

Remember that the following verbs are used before *that* and the verb word clause:

ask	prefer
demand	recommend
desire	require
insist	suggest

Avoid using a present or past verb instead of a verb word. Avoid using a modal before the verb word.

noun	that	S	verb word	
The recommendation	that	we	be	evaluated was approved

Remember that the following nouns are used in this pattern:

recommendation
requirement
suggestion

Avoid using a present or past verb instead of a verb word. Avoid using a modal before the verb word.

EXAMPLE:
Incorrect: The doctor suggested that she will not smoke.
Correct: The doctor *suggested* that she not *smoke.*

BASIC TIP 39   Impersonal expressions

it is	**adjective**		**infinitive**	
It is	important		to verify	the data
		or		
it is	**adjective**	**that**	**S**	**verb word**
It is	important	that	the data	be	verified

Remember that the following adjectives are used in this pattern:

> *essential*
> *imperative*
> *important*
> *necessary*

Avoid using a present verb instead of a verb word. Avoid using a modal before the verb word.

EXAMPLE:

Incorrect: It is not necessary that you must take an entrance examination to be admitted to an American university.

Correct: *It is not necessary to take* an entrance examination to be admitted to an American university.

         or

It is not necessary that you *take* an entrance examination to be admitted to an American university.

BASIC TIP 40   Causatives

S   HAVE someone verb word
My English teacher	had	us	give	oral reports
Avoid using an infinitive or an *-ing* form instead of a verb word before a person in patterns of cause.

S   MAKE   someone   verb word
His mother	made	him	take	his medicine
Avoid using an infinitive or an *-ing* form instead of a verb word before a person in patterns of cause.

S   HAVE   something   participle
I	want	to have	this book	renewed,	please
Avoid using a verb word or an infinitive instead of a participle before a thing in patterns of cause.

EXAMPLE:
  Incorrect: Tom had a tooth fill.
  Correct: Tom *had a tooth filled*.

BASIC TIP 41   Tag questions

Tag questions are used frequently in conversation to encourage agreement or to verify a statement.

Remember that the subject in the main clause and the subject in the tag question must refer to the same person or thing. The tag question is separated from the main clause by a comma.

S	BE	,	BE not	S
The mail	is	late,	isn't	it?

S	BE not	,	BE	S
The mail	isn't	late again,	is	it?

Avoid using a negative in both the main clause and the tag question.

S	V (present)	,	DO not	S
They	agree	with us,	don't	they?

Avoid using *won't* instead of *don't* or *doesn't*. Avoid using *did*.

S	V (past)	,	did not	S
They	agreed	with us,	didn't	they?

Avoid using *don't* or *doesn't* instead of *didn't*.

EXAMPLE:
  Incorrect: I owe you twenty dollars, won't I?
  Correct: *I owe* you twenty dollars, *don't I?*

BASIC TIP 42   More tag questions

S	will	verb word,	won't	S
You	will	help,	won't	you?
Avoid using *will* instead of *won't*.				
S	can	verb word,	can't	S
He	can	swim,	can't	he?
Avoid using *can* instead of *can't*.				
S	HAVE to	verb word,	DO not	S
We	have to	hurry,	don't	we?
Avoid using *HAVE not* instead of *DO not*.				
S	had to	verb word,	didn't	S
She	had to	leave,	didn't	she?
Avoid using *hadn't* instead of *didn't*.				
S	ought to	verb word,	shouldn't	S
I	ought to	complain,	shouldn't	I?
Avoid using the incorrect form *oughtn't* instead of *shouldn't*.				
Let's	verb word	,	shall	we
Let's	talk	about it,	shall	we?
Avoid using *doesn't* or *don't* instead of *shall*.				

EXAMPLE:
  Incorrect: We have to sign this, have we?
  Correct: *We have to* sign this, *don't we?*

BASIC TIP 43   **Ambiguous tag questions**

The abbreviation *'s* may refer to either *is* or *has*.				
S's	**-ing form**		**isn't**	**S**
She's	doing	her best,	isn't	she?
Avoid using *hasn't* instead of *isn't* when the abbreviation is followed by an *-ing* form.				
S's	**participle**	,	**hasn't**	**S**
She's	done	her best,	hasn't	she?
Avoid using *isn't* instead of *hasn't* when the abbreviation is followed by a participle.				

The abbreviation *'d* may refer to either *would* or *had*.				
S'd	**verb word**	,	**wouldn't**	**S**
He'd	work	overtime,	wouldn't	he?
Avoid using *hadn't* instead of *wouldn't* when the abbreviation is followed by a verb word.				
S'd	**participle**	,	**hadn't**	**S**
He'd	worked	overtime,	hadn't	he?
Avoid using *wouldn't* instead of *hadn't* when the abbreviation is followed by a participle.				

EXAMPLE:
  Incorrect: She's taken the test already, *isn't* she?
  Correct: She's *taken* the test already, *hasn't she?*

BASIC TIP 44   Affirmative agreement

S	BE		,	and	so	BE	S
They	were	surprised,	and	so	were	we	

Avoid using *also* instead of *so*. **Avoid using the incorrect pattern:**

S	BE		,	and	S	BE	so
They	were	surprised,	and	we	were	so	

S	V		,	and	so	DO	S
My wife	talked	to him about it,	and	so	did	I	

Avoid using *BE* instead of *DO*. Avoid using the verb again instead of *DO*. **Avoid using the incorrect pattern:**

S	V		,	and	S	DO	so
My wife	talked	to him about it,	and	— I	did	so	

EXAMPLE:
   Incorrect: We are going to the concert, and so do they.
   Correct: *We are going* to the concert, and *so are they*.

BASIC TIP 45   Negative agreement

S	MODAL HAVE DO BE not	verb word participle verb word -ing form,	and neither	MODAL HAVE DO BE	S
My roommate	won't	go,	and neither	will	I
My roommate	hasn't	gone,	and neither	have	I
My roommate	doesn't	go,	and neither	do	I
My roommate	isn't	going,	and neither	am	I

Avoid using *either* instead of *neither*. Avoid using the subject before *BE*, *DO*, *HAVE*, or the modal in a clause with *neither*.

S	MODAL HAVE DO BE not	verb word participle verb word -ing form,	and S	MODAL HAVE DO BE not	either
My roommate	won't	go,	and I	won't	either
My roommate	hasn't	gone,	and I	haven't	either
My roommate	doesn't	go,	and I	don't	either
My roommate	isn't	going,	and I	'm not	either

Avoid using *neither* instead of *either*.

EXAMPLE:

  Incorrect: She hasn't finished the assignment yet, and neither I have.

  Correct: She hasn't finished the assignment yet, and neither have I.

  or

  She hasn't finished the assignment yet, and I haven't either.

BASIC TIP 46   **Negative imperatives**

Please don't	**verb word**	
Please don't	tell	anyone
Avoid using an infinitive instead of a verb word.		
Would you please not	**verb word**	
Would you please not	tell	anyone
Avoid using an infinitive instead of a verb word. Avoid using *don't* after *would you please.*		

EXAMPLE:

    Incorrect: Would you please don't smoke?

    Correct: *Please don't smoke.*

                  or

                  Would you please not smoke?

BASIC TIP 47   -*Ing* forms modified by possessive pronouns

S	V Ph V	pronoun (possessive)	-*ing* form	
We	can count on	her	helping	us
He	regretted	their	misunderstanding	him

Remember that the following are possessive pronouns:

my	*our*
your	*your*
her	*their*
his	
its	

Avoid using subject or object pronouns between the verb and the -*ing* form.

EXAMPLE:

Incorrect: We don't understand why you object to him coming with us.

Correct: We don't understand why you object to *his coming* with us.

BASIC TIP 48   Subject and object pronouns

	pronoun (subject)	V	
If the weather is good,	Ellen and I	will go	to the beach

Remember that the following pronouns are subject pronouns:

I	we
you	you
she	they
he	
it	

Avoid using an object pronoun as a subject.

it	BE	pronoun (subject)	
It	is	he	whom the committee has named

Avoid using an object pronoun instead of a subject pronoun after the verb BE.

S V pronoun (object)
They asked us, Jane and me, whether we were satisfied
Remember that the following pronouns are object pronouns: me   us   you   you   her   them   him   it   Avoid using a subject pronoun as an object.
Let pronoun (object) V
Let us, you and me, try to reach an agreement
Avoid using a subject pronoun after *let*.

EXAMPLE:
Incorrect: It was her whom everyone wanted to win.
Correct: *It was she* whom everyone wanted to win.

BASIC TIP 49   Prepositions with object pronouns

	preposition	pronoun (object)
I would be glad to take a message	for	her

Remember that the following prepositions are commonly used with object pronouns:

among	of
between	to
for	with
from	

Avoid using a subject pronoun instead of an object pronoun after a preposition.

EXAMPLE:

Incorrect: The experiment proved to my lab partner and I that prejudices about the results of an investigation are often unfounded.

Correct: The experiment proved *to* my lab partner and *me* that prejudices about the results of an investigation are often unfounded.

BASIC TIP 50   **Relative pronouns which refer to persons**

who   V
Everyone who took the tour was impressed by the paintings
Avoid using *whom* as the subject of a verb.
whom   S   V
He was the only American whom I saw at the conference
Avoid using *who* instead of *whom* before a subject and a verb.

EXAMPLE:
  Incorrect: I asked him who he was calling.
  Correct: I asked him *whom he was calling.*

BASIC TIP 51   **Relative pronouns which refer to persons and things**

someone   who
She is the secretary who works in the international office
Avoid using *which* instead of *who* in reference to a person.
something   which
This is   the new typewriter   which   you ordered
Avoid using *who* instead of *which* in reference to a thing.

EXAMPLE:
  Incorrect: The people which cheated on the examination had to leave the room.
  Correct: The people who cheated on the examination had to leave the room.

BASIC TIP 52   Count and non-count nouns

few	
many	**noun (count)**

Few reference books	may be checked out
There are many television programs	for children on Saturday

Remember that the following nouns are examples of count nouns:

books	friends
classes	programs
dollars	seats

Avoid using a non-count noun instead of a count noun after *few* and *many*.

---

	little	**noun**
	much	**(non-count)**

Before he came to the U.S., he had done	little	traveling
We don't have	much	information

Remember that the following nouns are examples of non-count nouns:

advice	information
hair	money
homework	news

Avoid using a count noun instead of a non-count noun after *little* and *much*.

only a few noun (count)		
Only a few	dollars	have been budgeted for supplies
Avoid using *few* instead of *a few* after *only*.		
	only a little noun (non-count)	
We have	only a little	homework for Monday
Avoid using *little* instead of *a little* after *only*.		

EXAMPLE:

Incorrect: He had to balance his account very carefully because he had few money.

Correct: He had to balance his account very carefully because he had *little money*.

BASIC TIP 53   **Singular expressions of non-count nouns**

	a	singular	of	noun (non-count)
A folk song is	a	piece	of	popular music

Remember that the following singular expressions are idiomatic:

> *a piece of bread*
> *a piece of equipment*
> *a piece of furniture*
> *a piece of jewelry*
> *a piece of luggage*
> *a piece of mail*
> *a piece of music*
> *a piece of toast*
> *a loaf of bread*
> *a slice of bread*
> *an ear of corn*

EXAMPLE:

   Incorrect: A mail travels faster when the zip code is indicated on the envelope.

   Correct: *A piece of mail* travels faster when the zip code is indicated on the envelope.

BASIC TIP 54   Numbers with nouns

<table>
<tr><td colspan="3" align="center">**the   ordinal number   noun**</td></tr>
<tr><td>I am outlining the</td><td>sixth</td><td>chapter in my notebook</td></tr>
</table>

Remember that the following are ordinal numbers:

first	*eighth*	*fifteenth*
second	*ninth*	*sixteenth*
third	*tenth*	*seventeenth*
fourth	*eleventh*	*eighteenth*
fifth	*twelfth*	*nineteenth*
sixth	*thirteenth*	*twentieth*
seventh	*fourteenth*	

Avoid using *the* before the noun instead of before the ordinal number. Avoid using a cardinal instead of an ordinal number.

noun		**cardinal number**	
I am outlining	chapter	six	in my notebook

Remember that the following are cardinal numbers:

one	*eight*	*fifteen*
two	*nine*	*sixteen*
three	*ten*	*seventeen*
four	*eleven*	*eighteen*
five	*twelve*	*nineteen*
six	*thirteen*	*twenty*
seven	*fourteen*	

Avoid using *the* before the cardinal number or before the noun. Avoid using an ordinal number instead of a cardinal number.

EXAMPLE:

Incorrect: Flight 656 for Los Angeles is now ready for boarding at the concourse seven.

Correct: Flight 656 for Los Angeles is now ready for boarding at *concourse seven*.

BASIC TIP 55 **Nouns which function as adjectives**

Remember that when two nouns occur together, the first noun describes the second noun; that is, the first noun functions as an adjective.

	noun	noun
All of us are foreign	language	teachers

Avoid using a plural form for the first noun even when the second noun is plural. Avoid using a possessive form for the first noun.

EXAMPLE:
  Incorrect: May I borrow some notebooks paper?
  Correct: May I borrow some *notebook paper?*

BASIC TIP 56 **Hyphenated adjectives**

Remember that it is common for a number to appear as the first in a series of hyphenated adjectives.

a	adjective	—	adjective	noun
Agriculture 420 is a	five	—	hour	class

a adjective	—	adjective	—	adjective	noun
A sixty	—	year	—	old	employee may retire

Avoid using a plural form for any of the adjectives joined by hyphens even when the noun is plural.

EXAMPLE:

> *Incorrect:* A three-minutes call anywhere in the United
> States costs less than a dollar when you dial
> it yourself.
>
> *Correct:* A *three-minute call* anywhere in the United
> States costs less than a dollar when you dial
> it yourself.

BASIC TIP 57   Modifiers of cause in clauses of cause-and-result

S	V	so	adverb adjective	that	S	V
She	got up	so	late	that	she	missed her bus
The music	was	so	loud	that	we	couldn't talk

Avoid using *as* or *too* instead of *so*. Avoid using *as* instead of *that*.

EXAMPLE:

> *Incorrect:* He is so slow as he never gets to class on
> time.
>
> *Correct:* He is *so slow that* he never gets to class on
> time.

BASIC TIP 58   **More cause-and-result**

S	V	such	a	adjective	noun (singular)	that	S	V
It	was	such	a	lovely	day	that	we	went out

or

S	V	so	adjective	a	noun (singular)	that	S	V
It	was	so	lovely	a	day	that	we	went out

Avoid using *so* instead of *such* before *a*. Avoid omitting *a* from the patterns.

			noun (plural)			

noun (plural)
noun

S	V	such	adjective	noun (non-count)	that	S	V
These	are	such	long	assignments	that	I	can't finish them
This	is	such	good	news	that	I	will call them

Avoid using *so* instead of *such*.

EXAMPLE:
Incorrect: It was so interesting book that he couldn't put it down.
Correct: It was *such an interesting book* that he couldn't put it down.
         or
        It was *so interesting a book* that he couldn't put it down.

BASIC TIP 59   Sufficiency for a purpose

S	V	adjective	enough	infinitive	
It	is	warm	enough	to go	swimming

S	V	not	adjective	enough	infinitive	
It	is	not	warm	enough	to go	swimming

Avoid using *enough* before the adjective instead of after it.
Avoid using *as* between *enough* and the infinitive.

EXAMPLE:

Incorrect: Her little car isn't big enough as to seat more
than two people comfortably.

Correct: Her little car isn't *big enough* to seat more
than two people comfortably.

BASIC TIP 60   Adjectives with verbs of the senses

S	V (senses)	adjective	
I	felt	bad	about the mistake

Avoid using an adverb instead of an adjective after verbs of
the senses.

Remember that the following verbs are examples of verbs of
the senses:

feel	*smell*
look	*sound*
	taste

EXAMPLE:
Incorrect: We love to go to the country in the spring
because the wild flowers smell so sweetly.
Correct: We love to go to the country in the spring
because the wild flowers *smell* so *sweet*.

BASIC TIP 61   Adverbs of manner

S	V	adverb (manner)	
The class	listened	attentively	to the lecture

Remember that adverbs of manner describe the manner in
which the verb acts. Adverbs of manner usually end in *-ly*.

Avoid using an adjective instead of an adverb of manner.
Avoid using an adverb of manner between the two words of
an infinitive.

EXAMPLE:
Incorrect: After only six months in the United States,
Jack understood everyone perfect.
Correct: After only six months in the United States,
Jack understood everyone *perfectly*.

BASIC TIP 62   The adverbs of manner *fast* and *late*

S	V		fast
This medication	relieves	headache	fast

S	V		late
My roommate	returned	home	late last night

Remember that although most adverbs of manner end in *-ly*, *fast* and *late* do not have *-ly* endings.

Avoid using the **incorrect** forms *fastly* and *lately*.

EXAMPLE:
 Incorrect: Helen types fastly and efficiently.
 Correct: Helen types *fast* and efficiently.

BASIC TIP 63   Time modifiers

S	HAVE	participle			for	quantity of time
She	has	been	in the U.S.	for	six months

S	HAVE	participle			since	specific time
She	has	been	in the U.S.	since	June

S	HAVE participle			since quantity of time	ago
She	has	been	in the U.S. since	six months	ago

Remember that a quantity of time may be several days—a month, two years, etc. A specific time may be Wednesday, July, 1960, etc.

Avoid using *for* before specific times. Avoid using *for* with *ago*. Avoid using *before* after *HAVE* and a participle.

EXAMPLE:

   Incorrect: Mary has been on a diet since three weeks.

   Correct: Mary has been on a diet *for three weeks.*

                or

              Mary has been on a diet *since three weeks ago.*

BASIC TIP 64   **Dates**

	the	ordinal number	of	month
Valentines Day is on	the	fourteenth	of	February

Avoid using a cardinal number instead of an ordinal number after *the*. Avoid omitting *of* or *the* from the pattern.

EXAMPLE:

Incorrect: I have an appointment on the five of June at three o'clock.

Correct: I have an appointment on *the fifth of June* at three o'clock.

BASIC TIP 65   **Noun comparatives**

	noun	V	like	noun
I believe that	this coat	is	like	that one

Remember that *like* is a preposition. *As* is a conjunction. Avoid using *as* instead of *like* in prepositional phrases.

	noun	V	the same as	noun
I believe that	this coat	is	the same as	that one

Avoid using *to*, *that*, or *like* instead of *as* in the phrase with *the same*.

EXAMPLE:

Incorrect: That car is almost the same like mine.

Correct: That car is almost *like* mine.

or

That car is almost *the same as* mine.

BASIC TIP 66   **More noun comparatives**

noun	V	the same	noun (quality)	as	noun
She	is	the same	age	as	John

Remember that the following are examples of quality nouns:

age	price
color	size
height	style
length	weight

Avoid using *to, than,* or *like* instead of *as.* Avoid using a quality adjective instead of a quality noun after *the same.*

noun	V	as	adjective (quality)	as	noun
She	is	as	old	as	John

Remember that the following are examples of quality adjectives:

big	light
cheap	little
clear	long
easy	old
expensive	short
hard	small
heavy	tall
large	young

Avoid using *to, than,* or *like* instead of *as.* Avoid using a quality noun instead of a quality adjective after *as.*

EXAMPLE:
Incorrect: Mary worked as hard than Bill did.
Correct: Mary worked *as hard as* Bill did.

BASIC TIP 67   Pseudo-comparatives

Remember that although *as high as* and *as soon as* appear to be comparatives, they are idioms. *As high as* introduces a limit of height or cost. *As soon as* introduces a limit of time.

as high as		
The price of a haircut runs	as high as	five dollars

S	will	verb word	as soon as	S	V (present)
He	will	go home	as soon as	he	graduates

Avoid using *to* instead of *as*. Avoid using *will* and a verb word instead of a present verb after *as soon as*.

EXAMPLE:
Incorrect: I plan to move as soon as I will find another apartment.
Correct: I plan to move *as soon as I find* another apartment.

BASIC TIP 68   **Multiple comparatives**

	multiple	as	much many	as	
Fresh fruit costs	twice	as	much	as	canned fruit
We have	half	as	many	as	we need

Remember that the following are examples of multiple numbers:

half	four times
twice	five times
three times	

Avoid using *so* instead of *as* after a multiple. Avoid using *more than* instead of *as much as* or *as many as*. Avoid using the multiple after *as much as* and *as many as.*

EXAMPLE:

Incorrect: This one is prettier, but it costs twice more than the other one.

Correct: This one is prettier, but it costs *twice as much as* the other one.

BASIC TIP 69   **Comparatives and superlatives**

	more adjective/adverb adjective/adverb -er	than	
An essay test is	more difficult	than	an objective test
An essay test is	harder	than	an objective test

Remember that two- and three-syllable adjectives or adverbs form the comparative by using *more* before the adjective or adverb form. One-syllable adjectives or adverbs form the comparative by using *-er* after the form. Two-syllable adjectives or adverbs which end in *y* form the comparative by changing the *y* to *i* and adding *-er*.

Avoid using *as* or *that* instead of *than*. Avoid using both *more* and an *-er* form.

	the	most adjective/adverb adjective/adverb -est
An essay test is	the	most difficult
An essay test is	the	hardest

Remember that superlatives are used to compare more than two.

Avoid using a comparative *-er* form when three or more are compared.

EXAMPLE:
Incorrect: She is more prettier than all of the girls in our class.
Correct: She is *the prettiest* girl in our class.

BASIC TIP 70   Illogical comparatives

noun (singular)	more adjective adjective -er	than	that
The climate in the north is	more severe	than	that of the south
The climate in the north is	colder	than	that of the south

noun (plural)	more adjective adjective -er	than	those
The prices are	more expensive	than	those at a discount store
The prices are	higher	than	those at a discount store

noun (singular)	different	from	that
Football in the U.S. is	different	from	that of other countries

noun (plural)	different	from	those
The rules are	different	from	those of soccer

Remember that comparisons must be made with logically comparable nouns.

Avoid omitting *that* and *those*. Avoid using *than* instead of *from* with *different*.

EXAMPLE:
Incorrect: Her qualifications are better than any other candidate.
Correct: *Her qualifications* are *better than those* of any other candidate.

SIC TIP 71   Double comparatives

The comparative	S	V,	the comparative	S	V
The	more	you review, the	easier	the patterns will be

Remember that a comparative is *more* or *less* with an adjective, or an adjective with *-er*.

Avoid using *as* instead of *the*. Avoid using the **incorrect** form *lesser*. Avoid omitting *the*. Avoid omitting *-er* from the adjective.

EXAMPLE:

Incorrect: The more you study during the semester, the lesser you have to study the week before exams.

Correct: *The more* you study during the semester, *the less* you have to study the week before exams.

BASIC TIP 72   Inclusives and exclusives

	noun adjective	as well as	noun adjective
He enjoys playing	basketball	as well as	football
He is	intelligent	as well as	athletic

	noun adjective	and	noun adjective	as well as	noun adjective
He enjoys playing	soccer	and	baseball	as well as	tennis
He is	intelligent	and	artistic	as well as	athletic

	both	noun adjective	and	noun adjective	
	Both	Dr. Jones	and	Miss Smith	spoke
The lecture was	both	interesting	and	instructive	

Avoid using *as well as* instead of *and* with *both*. Avoid using *both . . . and* for more than two nouns or adjectives.

	not only	noun adjective	but also	noun adjective
One should take	not only	cash	but also	traveler's checks
Checks are	not only	safer	but also	more convenient

Avoid using *only not* instead of *not only*. Avoid using *but* instead of *but also*. **Avoid using the incorrect pattern:**

not only	noun adjective	but	noun adjective	also
	cash	but	traveler's checks	also
not only	safer	but	more convenient	also

	not	**noun** **adjective**	but	**noun** **adjective**
The largest university is	not	Minnesota	but	Ohio State
The school color is	not	blue	but	red

Avoid using *only* instead of *but*.

EXAMPLE:
> *Incorrect:* The program provides only not theoretical classes but also practical training.
>
> *Correct:* The program provides *not only* theoretical classes *but also* practical training.

BASIC TIP 73   Question words as connectors

S	**V**		**question word**	**S**	**V**
I	don't remember		what	her name	is

V	**S**		**question word**	**S**	**V**
Do	you	remember	what	her name	is?

Avoid using *do, does,* or *did* after the question word. Avoid using the verb before the subject after the question word.

EXAMPLE:
> *Incorrect:* I didn't understand what did he say.
>
> *Correct:* I didn't understand *what he said*.

BASIC TIP 74   **Purpose connectors**

S	V		so that	S	V	
He	is studying	hard	so that	he	can pass	his exams

Remember that although the form *so* is commonly used instead of *so that* in spoken English, it is not considered correct in written English.

Avoid using *so* instead of *so that* as a purpose connector in written English.

EXAMPLE:

Incorrect: He borrowed the money so he could finish his education.

Correct: He borrowed the money *so that* he could finish his education.

BASIC TIP 75   **Condition and unexpected result**

Despite	**noun,**	
Despite	his denial,	we knew that he was guilty

or

In spite of	**noun,**	
In spite of	his denial,	we knew that he was guilty

Avoid using *of* with *despite*. Avoid omitting *of* after *in spite*.

EXAMPLE:

Incorrect: Despite of the light rain, the baseball game was not canceled.

Correct: *Despite* the light rain, the baseball game was not canceled.

or

In spite of the light rain, the baseball game was not canceled.

BASIC TIP 76   Cause connectors

	because S V	
They decided to stay at home because the weather was bad		
. or		
	because of noun	
They decided to stay at home because of the weather		
Avoid using *because of* before a subject and verb. Avoid using *because* before a noun which is not followed by a verb.		

EXAMPLE:

Incorrect: Classes will be canceled tomorrow because a national holiday.

Correct: Classes will be canceled tomorrow *because it is* a national holiday.

or

Classes will be canceled tomorrow *because of* a national holiday.

Part B   Written Expression

BASIC TIP 77   Verbs

> In all patterns, maintain a point of view, either present or past.
>
> Avoid changing from present to past tense, or from past to present tense in the same sentence.

EXAMPLE:

Incorrect: He was among the few who want to continue working on the project.

Correct: He *is* among the few who *want* to continue working on the project.

or

He *was* among the few who *wanted* to continue working on the project.

BASIC TIP 78   More verbs

S	V (past)	that	S	V (past)	
He	said	that	he	was	sorry

Remember that the following verbs are used as the first past verb in the pattern above:

asked	reported
forgot	said
knew	thought
remembered	told

Avoid using a present verb after *that* in the pattern.

EXAMPLE:
Incorrect: I thought that he is coming today.
Correct: I *thought* that he *was* coming today.

BASIC TIP 79   Verbs and adverbs

> In all patterns, avoid using past adverbs with verbs in the
> present tense.

EXAMPLE:
Incorrect: Between one thing and another, Charles
does not finish typing his paper last night.
Correct: Between one thing and another, Charles *did*
not finish typing his paper *last night*.

BASIC TIP 80   Activities of the dead

> In all patterns, avoid using present verbs to refer to activities
> of the dead.

EXAMPLE:
Incorrect: Just before he died, my friend who writes
poetry published his first book.
Correct: *Just before he died*, my friend who *wrote*
poetry published his first book.

BASIC TIP 81   **Agreement of modified subject and verb**

> In all patterns, there must be agreement of subject and verb.
>
> Avoid using a verb which agrees with the modifier of a subject instead of with the subject itself.

EXAMPLE:

Incorrect: His knowledge of languages and international relations aid him in his work.

Correct: His *knowledge* of languages and international relations *aids* him in his work.

BASIC TIP 82   **Agreement of subject with accompaniment and verb**

> In all patterns, avoid using a verb which agrees with a phrase of accompaniment instead of with the subject itself.

EXAMPLE:

Incorrect: The guest of honor, along with his wife and two sons, were seated at the first table.

Correct: The *guest of honor,* along with his wife and two sons, *was seated* at the first table.

BASIC TIP 83   Verb-subject patterns

there	V	S
There	are	the results of the election
here	**V**	**S**
Here	is	the result of the election

Remember that *there* and *here* introduce verb-subject order.

Avoid using a verb that does not agree with the subject.

negative	auxiliary	S	V	
Never	have	I	seen	so much snow

Remember that negatives include phrases like *not one, not once, never again, only rarely,* and *very seldom.* Auxiliaries must agree with verbs.

Avoid using a subject before the auxiliary in this pattern.

EXAMPLE:
   Incorrect: There was ten people in line already when we arrived.
   Correct: There *were ten people* in line already when we arrived.

BASIC TIP 84   **Agreement of an indefinite or collective subject and verb**

Remember that the following subjects are singular:

anyone	neither
anything	no one
each	nothing
either	what
everyone	whatever
everything	whoever

The following subjects are plural:

> few
> people
> the rest

Avoid using plural verbs with singular subjects, and singular verbs with plural subjects.

EXAMPLE:

Incorrect: Everyone who majors in architecture and fine arts study History of Art 450.

Correct: Everyone who majors in architecture and fine arts *studies* History of Art 450.

BASIC TIP 85   **Agreement of noun and pronoun**

In all patterns, there must be agreement of noun and pronoun.

Avoid using a pronoun that does not agree with the noun to which it refers.

EXAMPLE:

> *Incorrect:* Those of us who are over fifty years old should get their blood pressure checked regularly.
>
> *Correct:* *Those of us* who are over fifty years old should get *our* blood pressure checked regularly.

BASIC TIP 86   **Agreement of subject and possessive pronouns**

In all patterns, there must be agreement of subject pronoun and possessive pronouns which refer to the subject.

Remember that the following possessive pronouns are singular:

> *her*
> *his*
> *its*

Avoid using *their* instead of *her, his,* or *its* when referring to a singular subject pronoun. Avoid using *her* instead of *his* unless referring specifically to a woman.

Note: The cultural catalyst of the women's movement along with the historical tendency toward a simplification of gender inflections in the English language has left authorities in disagreement as to whether or to what extent the gender of pronouns should be identified. Until some statement has been generally adopted, the pronoun patterns in this Review will be adequate for TOEFL preparation.

EXAMPLE:

Incorrect: Each student should have their schedule signed by the department chairman.

Correct: Each student should have *his* schedule signed by the department chairman.

BASIC TIP 87   Agreement of impersonal pronouns

In all patterns, there must be agreement of impersonal pronouns in a sentence.

Remember that for formal writing, it is necessary to continue using the impersonal pronoun *one* throughout a sentence. For more informal writing, *he* or *his* may be used instead of *one* or *one's*.

Avoid using *you, your, they*, or *their* to refer to the impersonal pronoun *one*.

EXAMPLE:

Incorrect: At a large university, one will almost always be able to find a friend who speaks your language.

Correct: At a large university, *one* will almost always be able to find a friend who speaks *one's* language.

or

At a large university, *one* will almost always be able to find a friend who speaks *his* language.

BASIC TIP 88   Illogical modifiers

An introductory verbal modifier should immediately precede the noun which it modifies.

Avoid using a noun immediately after an introductory verbal phrase which may not be logically modified by the phrase. Avoid using a passive construction after an introductory verbal modifier.

EXAMPLE:

Incorrect: After graduating from City College, Professor Baker's studies were continued at State University where he received his Ph.D. in English.

Correct: *After graduating* from City College, *Professor Baker* continued his studies at State University where he received his Ph.D. in English.

BASIC TIP 89   **Parallel structure in a series**

> In all patterns, ideas of equal importance should be expressed by the same grammatical structure.
>
> Avoid expressing ideas in a series by different structures.

EXAMPLE:

Incorrect: Jane is young, enthusiastic, and she has talent.

Correct: Jane is *young, enthusiastic,* and *talented.*

BASIC TIP 90   **Parallel structure after inclusives**

> Avoid expressing ideas after inclusives by different structures.

EXAMPLE:

Incorrect: She is not only famous in the United States, but also abroad.

Correct: She is famous not only *in the United States,* but also *abroad.*

BASIC TIP 91   Unnecessary words

S	V	C
Vitamin C	prevents	colds
Anticipatory *it* clause	S	V	C
It is believed that	vitamin C	prevents	colds
Nominal *that* clause	V	
That vitamin C prevents colds	is	well known

Remember that an anticipatory *it* clause introduces a subject and verb. A nominal *that* clause introduces a verb or verb phrase.

Avoid using a combination of anticipatory *it* and nominal *that* in the same clause.

Avoid using an adjective with such phrases as *in character* or *in nature*.

Avoid using the wordy pattern in a adjective manner
in a quick manner
instead of an adverb such as *quickly*.

In all patterns, prefer simple, direct sentences to complicated, indirect sentences. Find the Subject-Verb-Complement and determine whether the other words are useful or unnecessary.

EXAMPLE:

Incorrect: That it is she has known him for a long time influenced her decision.

Correct: That she has known him for a long time influenced her decision.

BASIC TIP 92   Repetition of words with the same meaning

> In all patterns, avoid using words with the same meaning consecutively in a sentence.

EXAMPLE:

Incorrect: The new innovations at the World's Fair were fascinating.

Correct: The *innovations* at the World's Fair were fascinating.

BASIC TIP 93   Repetition of noun by pronoun

> In all patterns, avoid using a noun and the pronoun that refers to it consecutively in a sentence.

EXAMPLE:

Incorrect: My teacher he said to listen to the news on the radio in order to practice listening comprehension.

Correct: *My teacher said* to listen to the news on the radio in order to practice listening comprehension.

BASIC TIP 94   Confusing verbs

In all patterns, words should be chosen to express the exact meaning that the writer wishes to convey.

S	RAISE	C	M
Heavy rain	raises	the water level of the reservoir	every spring
Heavy rain	raised	the water level of the reservoir	last week

S	RISE	C	M
The water level	rises		when it rains every spring
The water level	rose		when it rained last week

Remember that *to raise* means to move to a higher place or to cause to rise. *To rise* means to go up or to increase.

S	LAY	C	M
The postman	lays	the mail	on the table every day
The postman	laid	the mail	on the table yesterday

S	LIE	C	M
He	lies		on the sofa to rest every day after work
He	lay		on the sofa to rest yesterday after work

Remember that *to lay* means to put, to place or to cause to lie. *To lie* means to recline or to occupy a place.

The past form of the verb *to lie* is *lay*.

S	LET	C	M
Their mother	lets	them	stay up late every night
Their mother	let	them	stay up late last night

S	LEAVE	C	M
She	leaves	work	to pick up the children at two o'clock every day
She	left	work	to pick up the children at two o'clock yesterday

Remember that *to let* means to allow or to permit. *To leave* means to depart or to go.

EXAMPLE:

Incorrect: The cost of living has raised over 8 percent in the past year.

Correct: The cost of living has *risen* over 8 percent in the past year.

BASIC TIP 95   Prepositional idioms

Avoid these errors	Prefer these idioms
accede on, by	accede to
according	according to
approve for	approve of
ashamed with	ashamed of
bored of	bored with
capable to	capable of
compare to	compare with
compete together	compete
composed from	composed of
concerned of	concerned with
conscious for	conscious of
effects in	effects on
equal as	equal to
excepting for	except for
after now on	from now on
frown to	frown on
glance	glance at, through
incapable to	incapable of
on conflict	in conflict
inferior with	inferior to
in the habit to	in the habit of
at the near future	in the near future
knowledge on	knowledge of
near to	near; next to
in opinion	of the opinion
opposite over	opposite
regard of	regard to
related with	related to
respect of	respect for

BASIC TIP 95   *(Continued)*

Avoid these errors	Prefer these idioms
similar as	similar to
ever since	since
surprised at	suprised by
up until	until
with regard of	with regard to

EXAMPLE:

Incorrect: Excepting for the Gulf Coast region, most of the nation will have very pleasant weather tonight and tomorrow.

Correct: *Except for* the Gulf Coast region, most of the nation will have very pleasant weather tonight and tomorrow.

BASIC TIP 96   **Parts of speech**

Abstract nouns derived from verbs often have the following endings: *-ation, -ity,* and *-ment.*

Remember that adjectives may not be used in place of nouns.

Avoid using adjectives that end in *-ing* and *-able* in place of abstract nouns. Avoid using verbs in place of nouns.

EXAMPLE:

Incorrect: The agreeing is not legal unless everyone signs his name.

Correct: The *agreement* is not legal unless everyone signs his name.

4

Basic Tips for Section III: Reading Comprehension and Vocabulary

Part A Vocabulary

BASIC TIP 97 **Vocabulary in context**

The Vocabulary Section of the TOEFL is probably the most difficult section to prepare for. Since there are hundreds, even thousands of words that may be tested, it is not possible to identify and study them all.

The Vocabulary Review in *Barron's How to Prepare for the TOEFL (Test of English as a Foreign Language)* contains a list of more than seven hundred words that are commonly tested on the TOEFL.

If you cannot study the Barron's list, you should develop your own list. Whenever you read formal English, such as a passage from a textbook or a magazine, copy sentences that have unfamiliar words in them onto cards or small slips of paper. Then write the same sentences with definitions of the new words on the back of the cards or paper.

Because vocabulary on the TOEFL is vocabulary in the context of a sentence, it is important to copy the sentences in which the words appear.

Keep some of the cards in your shirt pocket or in your purse. When you have time during the day, shuffle the cards and review the sentences. Concentrate on the words that you have seen more than one time in your reading.

In this simple way, you will soon know the most important words on your list.

EXAMPLE:
Front: The sound of the wind *abated*.
Back: The sound of the wind *decreased*.

Part B   Reading Comprehension

BASIC TIP 98   **Main Ideas**

The *main idea* is the most important point or idea in a reading passage. It is a general statement.

A main idea usually occurs at the beginning of a passage, either as a title or a topic sentence. Sometimes it is repeated at the end as a summary.

Answers to questions about main ideas may require a statement of the idea or a title that summarizes the main idea.

Some students prefer to answer the questions about main ideas first while they still have a general idea of the passage. Answering questions about details first can cause the reader to forget the main idea.

In reading for the main idea, use your skimming skills.

EXAMPLE:

Although dinosaurs have long captured man's imagination, no human ever saw one. For over one hundred million years dinosaurs roamed the earth, but for some unknown reason, they perished seventy million years ago, years before man appeared.

There are several theories as to why the giants disappeared. Some scientists believe that the earth became too cold; others believe that it became too dry; still others argue that smaller mammals ate the dinosaur eggs before they had an opportunity to hatch.

Whatever the reason, their great bodies sank into the mud where slowly the bones, teeth, and even the skin became fossilized. Today huge stone footprints and enormous skeletal structures are the only record we have of their mysterious existence.

Question: What is a good title for this passage?
Answer: The Disappearance of Dinosaurs.

BASIC TIP 99   Details

A *detail* is a specific fact. It may be an example or a statement to support the main idea.

Details usually occur after a main idea in a reading passage.

Answers to questions about details may require specific information about *who, what, when, where, why, how, how much,* or *how many,* etc.

In reading for details, use your scanning skills.

EXAMPLE:
    For fast relief of acid indigestion, heartburn and sour stomach due to acidity caused by eating or drinking in excess.
    Directions: Chew one or two tablets after meals and at bedtime, or as directed by a physician.
    Warning: Do not take more than 16 tablets in a 24-hour period or use the maximum dosage of this product for more than two weeks, except under the advice and supervision of a physician. Keep this and all drugs out of the reach of children.

Question: How do you take this medication?
Answer: You chew it.

BASIC TIP 100   **Inferences**

An *inference* is a logical conclusion.

An inference must be based on information in the reading passage, not on experience or information from other sources.

Answers to inference questions may require an interpretation or a prediction.

In reading for inferences, use your logic.

EXAMPLE:

Some government agencies or banks may require a statement concerning the cost of a student's education in the United States. In order to fulfill this requirement, State University students may present the following estimate to any authority needing such information:

Tuition and fees	$2400
Books and supplies	$ 400
Room and board	$4000
Insurance	$ 200
Miscellaneous	$1000
*Total	$8000

Question: Where would this information most probably be printed?

Answer: In a university catalog or an announcement published by State University.

* Estimate for one academic year or nine months, subject to change without notice.

BASIC TIP 101   Restatements

A *restatement* is a sentence that has the same meaning as another sentence.

Certain structures are more common as restatements, including passives, negatives, chronologies, comparatives, conditionals, and concessions.

In reading for restatements, use your knowledge of structure.

EXAMPLE:

Passive statement:	Because of death and divorce, about 17 percent of all children in the U.S. are brought up by only one parent.
Restatement:	Single parents bring up 17 percent of all children in the U.S.
Negative statement:	There have been only twenty-six days in recorded history in which a war was not going on somewhere in the world.
Restatement:	A war has been going on somewhere in the world for all but twenty-six days in recorded history.
Chronological statement:	Before Florida was traded to the English for Cuba, it belonged to the Spanish Empire.

Restatement: Florida belonged to the English after the Spanish traded it for Cuba.

Comparative statement: Since you may live for more than a week without food and three days without water, but only a few hours in severe weather, exposure to the elements is more dangerous than hunger and thirst.

Restatement: Hunger and thirst are less dangerous than exposure to the elements because you can live longer without food and water than you can in severe weather.

Conditional statement: If a *Y* chromosome is transferred from the father, the baby will be a boy.

Restatement: Male children are born when the father transfers a *Y* chromosome.

Concessional statement: Men don't usually shake hands with women in the United States unless they meet in a business situation or the woman offers her hand first.

Restatement: Men will shake hands with women in the United States if they meet in a business situation or if the woman offers her hand first.

Answer Sheet—Model Test 1

Section I: Listening Comprehension

1. Ⓐ Ⓑ Ⓒ Ⓓ
2. Ⓐ Ⓑ Ⓒ Ⓓ
3. Ⓐ Ⓑ Ⓒ Ⓓ
4. Ⓐ Ⓑ Ⓒ Ⓓ
5. Ⓐ Ⓑ Ⓒ Ⓓ
6. Ⓐ Ⓑ Ⓒ Ⓓ
7. Ⓐ Ⓑ Ⓒ Ⓓ
8. Ⓐ Ⓑ Ⓒ Ⓓ
9. Ⓐ Ⓑ Ⓒ Ⓓ
10. Ⓐ Ⓑ Ⓒ Ⓓ
11. Ⓐ Ⓑ Ⓒ Ⓓ
12. Ⓐ Ⓑ Ⓒ Ⓓ
13. Ⓐ Ⓑ Ⓒ Ⓓ
14. Ⓐ Ⓑ Ⓒ Ⓓ
15. Ⓐ Ⓑ Ⓒ Ⓓ
16. Ⓐ Ⓑ Ⓒ Ⓓ
17. Ⓐ Ⓑ Ⓒ Ⓓ
18. Ⓐ Ⓑ Ⓒ Ⓓ
19. Ⓐ Ⓑ Ⓒ Ⓓ
20. Ⓐ Ⓑ Ⓒ Ⓓ
21. Ⓐ Ⓑ Ⓒ Ⓓ
22. Ⓐ Ⓑ Ⓒ Ⓓ
23. Ⓐ Ⓑ Ⓒ Ⓓ
24. Ⓐ Ⓑ Ⓒ Ⓓ
25. Ⓐ Ⓑ Ⓒ Ⓓ
26. Ⓐ Ⓑ Ⓒ Ⓓ
27. Ⓐ Ⓑ Ⓒ Ⓓ
28. Ⓐ Ⓑ Ⓒ Ⓓ
29. Ⓐ Ⓑ Ⓒ Ⓓ
30. Ⓐ Ⓑ Ⓒ Ⓓ
31. Ⓐ Ⓑ Ⓒ Ⓓ
32. Ⓐ Ⓑ Ⓒ Ⓓ

33. Ⓐ Ⓑ Ⓒ Ⓓ
34. Ⓐ Ⓑ Ⓒ Ⓓ
35. Ⓐ Ⓑ Ⓒ Ⓓ
36. Ⓐ Ⓑ Ⓒ Ⓓ
37. Ⓐ Ⓑ Ⓒ Ⓓ
38. Ⓐ Ⓑ Ⓒ Ⓓ
39. Ⓐ Ⓑ Ⓒ Ⓓ
40. Ⓐ Ⓑ Ⓒ Ⓓ
41. Ⓐ Ⓑ Ⓒ Ⓓ
42. Ⓐ Ⓑ Ⓒ Ⓓ
43. Ⓐ Ⓑ Ⓒ Ⓓ
44. Ⓐ Ⓑ Ⓒ Ⓓ
45. Ⓐ Ⓑ Ⓒ Ⓓ
46. Ⓐ Ⓑ Ⓒ Ⓓ
47. Ⓐ Ⓑ Ⓒ Ⓓ
48. Ⓐ Ⓑ Ⓒ Ⓓ
49. Ⓐ Ⓑ Ⓒ Ⓓ
50. Ⓐ Ⓑ Ⓒ Ⓓ

Section II: Structure and Written Expression

1. Ⓐ Ⓑ Ⓒ Ⓓ
2. Ⓐ Ⓑ Ⓒ Ⓓ
3. Ⓐ Ⓑ Ⓒ Ⓓ
4. Ⓐ Ⓑ Ⓒ Ⓓ
5. Ⓐ Ⓑ Ⓒ Ⓓ
6. Ⓐ Ⓑ Ⓒ Ⓓ
7. Ⓐ Ⓑ Ⓒ Ⓓ
8. Ⓐ Ⓑ Ⓒ Ⓓ
9. Ⓐ Ⓑ Ⓒ Ⓓ
10. Ⓐ Ⓑ Ⓒ Ⓓ
11. Ⓐ Ⓑ Ⓒ Ⓓ
12. Ⓐ Ⓑ Ⓒ Ⓓ
13. Ⓐ Ⓑ Ⓒ Ⓓ
14. Ⓐ Ⓑ Ⓒ Ⓓ
15. Ⓐ Ⓑ Ⓒ Ⓓ
16. Ⓐ Ⓑ Ⓒ Ⓓ
17. Ⓐ Ⓑ Ⓒ Ⓓ
18. Ⓐ Ⓑ Ⓒ Ⓓ
19. Ⓐ Ⓑ Ⓒ Ⓓ
20. Ⓐ Ⓑ Ⓒ Ⓓ
21. Ⓐ Ⓑ Ⓒ Ⓓ
22. Ⓐ Ⓑ Ⓒ Ⓓ
23. Ⓐ Ⓑ Ⓒ Ⓓ
24. Ⓐ Ⓑ Ⓒ Ⓓ
25. Ⓐ Ⓑ Ⓒ Ⓓ
26. Ⓐ Ⓑ Ⓒ Ⓓ
27. Ⓐ Ⓑ Ⓒ Ⓓ
28. Ⓐ Ⓑ Ⓒ Ⓓ
29. Ⓐ Ⓑ Ⓒ Ⓓ
30. Ⓐ Ⓑ Ⓒ Ⓓ
31. Ⓐ Ⓑ Ⓒ Ⓓ
32. Ⓐ Ⓑ Ⓒ Ⓓ
33. Ⓐ Ⓑ Ⓒ Ⓓ
34. Ⓐ Ⓑ Ⓒ Ⓓ
35. Ⓐ Ⓑ Ⓒ Ⓓ
36. Ⓐ Ⓑ Ⓒ Ⓓ
37. Ⓐ Ⓑ Ⓒ Ⓓ
38. Ⓐ Ⓑ Ⓒ Ⓓ
39. Ⓐ Ⓑ Ⓒ Ⓓ
40. Ⓐ Ⓑ Ⓒ Ⓓ

Section III: Reading Comprehension and Vocabulary

1. (A) (B) (C) (D)
2. (A) (B) (C) (D)
3. (A) (B) (C) (D)
4. (A) (B) (C) (D)
5. (A) (B) (C) (D)
6. (A) (B) (C) (D)
7. (A) (B) (C) (D)
8. (A) (B) (C) (D)
9. (A) (B) (C) (D)
10. (A) (B) (C) (D)
11. (A) (B) (C) (D)
12. (A) (B) (C) (D)
13. (A) (B) (C) (D)
14. (A) (B) (C) (D)
15. (A) (B) (C) (D)
16. (A) (B) (C) (D)
17. (A) (B) (C) (D)
18. (A) (B) (C) (D)
19. (A) (B) (C) (D)
20. (A) (B) (C) (D)
21. (A) (B) (C) (D)
22. (A) (B) (C) (D)
23. (A) (B) (C) (D)
24. (A) (B) (C) (D)
25. (A) (B) (C) (D)
26. (A) (B) (C) (D)
27. (A) (B) (C) (D)
28. (A) (B) (C) (D)
29. (A) (B) (C) (D)
30. (A) (B) (C) (D)

31. (A) (B) (C) (D)
32. (A) (B) (C) (D)
33. (A) (B) (C) (D)
34. (A) (B) (C) (D)
35. (A) (B) (C) (D)
36. (A) (B) (C) (D)
37. (A) (B) (C) (D)
38. (A) (B) (C) (D)
39. (A) (B) (C) (D)
40. (A) (B) (C) (D)
41. (A) (B) (C) (D)
42. (A) (B) (C) (D)
43. (A) (B) (C) (D)
44. (A) (B) (C) (D)
45. (A) (B) (C) (D)
46. (A) (B) (C) (D)
47. (A) (B) (C) (D)
48. (A) (B) (C) (D)
49. (A) (B) (C) (D)
50. (A) (B) (C) (D)
51. (A) (B) (C) (D)
52. (A) (B) (C) (D)
53. (A) (B) (C) (D)
54. (A) (B) (C) (D)
55. (A) (B) (C) (D)
56. (A) (B) (C) (D)
57. (A) (B) (C) (D)
58. (A) (B) (C) (D)
59. (A) (B) (C) (D)
60. (A) (B) (C) (D)

Model Test 1

The Test

SECTION I: LISTENING COMPREHENSION

In this section of the test, you will have an opportunity to demonstrate your ability to understand spoken English. It is in three parts, and there are special directions for each part.

Note: The transcript for the Listening Comprehension Section can be found on page 141.

Part A

Directions: For each problem in Part A, you will hear a short statement. The statements will be *spoken* just one time. They will not be written out for you, and you must listen carefully in order to understand what the speaker says.

When you hear a statement, read the four sentences in your test book and decide which one is closest in meaning to the statement you have heard. Then, on your answer sheet, find the number of the problem and mark your answer.

1. (A) State University is new this year.
   (B) State University has been a public institution for fifteen years.
   (C) Fifty years ago State University became a state institution.
   (D) There are fifty universities in the state.

2. (A) The weather was nice this afternoon.
   (B) It usually rains in the afternoon.
   (C) Although we had expected rain, it was a nice day.
   (D) It rained in the afternoon.

3. (A) Mrs. Jones's neighbors are going to move to Florida.
   (B) Mrs. Jones is planning to move to Florida with her neighbors.
   (C) Mrs. Jones and her neighbors live in Florida.
   (D) I knew that Mrs. Jones had moved to Florida because her neighbors told me.

4. (A) I will take a present to the funeral.
   (B) I want to go to the funeral.
   (C) I will not go to the funeral.
   (D) I will go to the funeral because I have to attend.

5. (A) Tom knew about the party although no one told him.
   (B) Tom told her about the party because he did not know that it was a surprise.
   (C) Tom did not know about the party because it was a surprise.
   (D) Tom was surprised at the party.

6. (A) A new car costs two thousand dollars.
   (B) John did not plan to buy a used car.
   (C) John's car cost four thousand dollars.
   (D) Since a new car was too expensive, John decided to buy a used one.

7. (A) He is an average student.
   (B) He always gets A's.
   (C) He is French.
   (D) He received a C this term.

8. (A) For help, wait for an operator to answer.
   (B) For help, dial nine.
   (C) For help, answer the operator.
   (D) For help, stand in line.

9. (A) Miss Smith is one of the best instructors because she has taught longer.
   (B) Miss Smith is one of the best instructors in spite of her having less experience.
   (C) Other members of the staff teach less than Miss Smith does.
   (D) Miss Smith has the best experience of all of the instructors on the staff.

10. (A) I feel well now.
    (B) I felt better before.
    (C) I have never felt well.
    (D) I have always felt well.

11. (A) The paper boy is usually late.
    (B) It is after five o'clock now.
    (C) Today the paper boy came at five o'clock.
    (D) The paper boy has not come lately.

12. (A) Thirty people came.
    (B) We had ninety chairs.
    (C) Sixty people had to stand up.
    (D) We expected ninety people.

13. (A) Steve's brother is more handsome.
    (B) Steve looks like his brother.
    (C) Girls prefer Steve's brother.
    (D) Steve and his brother are more popular than the girls.

14. (A) There are two people in the club.
    (B) There are five people in the club.
    (C) There are ten people in the club.
    (D) There are thirty people in the club.

15. (A) Mary lived in Europe for two years.
    (B) Mary had to work for two years to take a vacation in Europe.
    (C) Mary took a vacation to Europe two years ago.
    (D) Mary did not go on vacation because she could not save enough money.

16. (A) We had planned to arrive at one o'clock.
    (B) We were delayed for four hours.
    (C) We were supposed to arrive at three o'clock.
    (D) We arrived at seven o'clock.

17. (A) I sew as well as Jane does.
    (B) Jane makes our clothes.
    (C) I own more clothes than Jane does.
    (D) I do not make my clothes because I do not sew well.

18. (A) We went to the basketball game but not to the disco.
    (B) We went to the basketball game first, and the disco later.
    (C) We went to the disco but not to the basketball game.
    (D) We did not go to the basketball game or to the disco.

19. (A) I am very concerned about pets.
    (B) I think that pets should live in the house.
    (C) In my opinion pets should be kept outside.
    (D) Some pets belong in the house and others belong outside.

20. (A) She was sorry that she had apologized.
    (B) She was sorry, but she did not apologize.
    (C) She was not sorry, but she apologized.
    (D) She was sorry that she did not apologize.

Part B

Directions: In Part B you will hear 15 short conversations between two speakers. At the end of each conversation, a third voice will ask a question about what was said. The question will be *spoken* just one time. After you hear a conversation and the question about it, read the four possible answers and decide which would be the best response to the question you have heard. Then, on your answer sheet, find the number of the question and mark your answer.

21. (A) It cost a nickel a gallon.
   (B) It cost 55 cents a gallon.
   (C) It cost 60 cents a gallon.
   (D) It cost 65 cents a gallon.

22. (A) In a flower shop.
   (B) In a hospital.
   (C) In a garden.
   (D) In a boat.

23. (A) They have spent the summer in Zimbabwe.
   (B) They are both from Africa.
   (C) They are sisters.
   (D) They are interested in art.

24. (A) She does not know how to play tennis.
   (B) She has to study.
   (C) She does not like the man.
   (D) She does not qualify to play.

25. (A) Because the other bakery does not have cake.
   (B) Because the other bakery is closed.
   (C) Because her mother owns the bakery on Wells Street.
   (D) Because it is the best bakery.

26. (A) He is a librarian.
   (B) He is a professor.
   (C) He is an accountant.
   (D) He is a reporter.

27. (A) $.75.
   (B) $1.00.
   (C) $3.25.
   (D) $5.00.

28. (A) He is studying at the American Language Institute.
   (B) He is taking three classes at the university.
   (C) He is a part-time student.
   (D) He is surprised.

29. (A) At the office.
   (B) At home.
   (C) On the way to the bank.
   (D) With her husband.

30. (A) Doctor-patient.
   (B) Dentist-patient.
   (C) Baker-customer.
   (D) Mechanic-customer.

31. (A) In Florida.
   (B) At the lake.
   (C) At a beauty shop.
   (D) At a skating rink.

32. (A) That Mr. Adams is the new foreign student advisor.
   (B) That the foreign student advisor is a man.
   (C) That the foreign student advisor is married.
   (D) That the foreign student advisor is not here.

33. (A) That she did not get a letter from her family today.
   (B) That she got a letter from her family two days ago.
   (C) That she got a letter from her family today.
   (D) That she does not expect to get any letters from her family.

34. (A) What the flight number is.
   (B) What time the flight departs.
   (C) Where to find a telephone.
   (D) Where to board the plane.

35. (A) A history book.
   (B) A math book.
   (C) An English book.
   (D) A music book.

Part C

Directions: In this part of the test, you will hear several short talks and conversations. After each talk or conversation, you will be asked some questions. The talks and questions will be *spoken* just one time. They will not be written out for you, so you will have to listen carefully in order to understand and remember what the speaker says.

When you hear a question, read the four possible answers in your test book and decide which one would be the best answer to the question you have heard. Then, on your answer sheet, find the number of the problem and fill in (blacken) the space that corresponds to the letter of the answer you have chosen.

MINI-TALK ONE

36. (A) They described the Jazz Age.
    (B) They described the deep South.
    (C) They were based upon war experiences.
    (D) They were written in stream-of-consciousness style.

37. (A) In 1940.
    (B) After his death.
    (C) In 1925.
    (D) When he wrote the novel *Tender is the Night*.

38. (A) *Tender is the Night*.
    (B) *All the Sad Young Men*.
    (C) *The Great Gatsby*.
    (D) *Zelda Sayre*.

39. (A) He had little natural talent.
    (B) He was a compulsive drinker.
    (C) He improved his work as a mature writer.
    (D) He adjusted to a changing world.

40. (A) In 1940.
    (B) The same year in which he married Zelda Sayre.
    (C) In 1925.
    (D) In the same year in which he died.

MINI-TALK TWO

41. (A) Detroit Metro Airport.
    (B) Toledo Express Airport.
    (C) Columbus International Airport.
    (D) Chicago O'Hare Airport.

42. (A) They should go to the Greater Cincinnati Airport.
    (B) They should call the airport to be certain that their flight is scheduled to depart.
    (C) They should cancel their travel plans.
    (D) They should stay tuned to their radios.

43. (A) Severe wind.
    (B) Heavy fog.
    (C) Thunder storms.
    (D) Snow storms.

MINI-TALK THREE

44. (A) The woman's husband.
    (B) The owner of the apartment.
    (C) The apartment manager.
    (D) The tenant who occupies the apartment now.

45. (A) In a house.
    (B) In a hotel.
    (C) In a two-bedroom apartment.
    (D) In a three-bedroom apartment.

46. (A) Because she thought the apartment was too small.
    (B) Because it was the first apartment she had seen.
    (C) Because her husband had not seen it.
    (D) Because the rent was too high.

MINI-TALK FOUR

47. (A) Health food.
    (B) The processing of bread.
    (C) Organic gardens.
    (D) Poisons.

48. (A) Refined foods.
    (B) Natural foods.
    (C) Organic foods.
    (D) Unprocessed foods.

49. (A)   They are all used to keep the bread from getting moldy.
   (B)   They are all poisons.
   (C)   They are all organic.
   (D)   They have all killed laboratory animals.

50. (A)   The ultimate content remains the same.
   (B)   Vitamin information is not available after processing.
   (C)   Vitamins are added to the food.
   (D)   The vitamin content is reduced.

STOP. IF YOU HAVE FINISHED BEFORE TIME IS CALLED, CHECK YOUR WORK ON THIS SECTION ONLY. DO NOT WORK ON ANY OTHER SECTION OF THE TEST.

SECTION II: STRUCTURE AND WRITTEN EXPRESSION

40 QUESTIONS
25 MINUTES

Part A

Directions: In Part A each problem consists of an incomplete sentence. Four words or phrases, marked (A), (B), (C), (D), are given beneath the sentence. You are to choose the *one* word or phrase that best completes the sentence. Then, on your answer sheet, find the number of the problem and mark your answer.

1. It is important that the TOEFL Office _____ your registration.
   - (A) will confirm
   - (B) confirm
   - (C) confirms
   - (D) must confirm

2. As a safety precaution, all city cab drivers carry only enough money to make change for a _____ bill.
   - (A) ten-dollar
   - (B) ten-dollars
   - (C) tens-dollar
   - (D) tens-dollars

3. _____ that the English settled in Jamestown.
   - (A) In 1607 that it was
   - (B) That in 1607
   - (C) Because in 1607
   - (D) It was in 1607

4. Staying in a hotel costs _____ renting a room in a dormitory for a week.
   - (A) twice more than
   - (B) twice as much as
   - (C) as much twice as
   - (D) as much as twice

5. When friends insist on _____ expensive gifts, it makes most Americans uncomfortable.
   - (A) them to accept
   - (B) their accepting
   - (C) they accepting
   - (D) they accept

6. Gilbert Stuart is considered by most art critics _____ greatest portrait painter in the North American colonies.
   - (A) that he was
   - (B) as he was
   - (C) who was the
   - (D) the

7. As a safety measure, the detonator for a nuclear device may be made of _____ each of which is controlled by a different employee.
   (A) two equipments
   (B) two pieces of equipments
   (C) two pieces of equipment
   (D) two equipment pieces

8. A student should tell a dorm counselor if _____ live with his roommate again next year.
   (A) he'd rather not   (C) he'll rather not
   (B) he won't rather   (D) he'd rather didn't

9. It is the first time that the Princess of Wales has been to the United States, _____?
   (A) isn't she   (C) isn't it
   (B) hasn't she   (D) hasn't it

10. _____ two waves pass a given point simultaneously, they will have no effect on each other's subsequent motion.
   (A) So that   (C) That
   (B) They are   (D) If

11. A child in the first grade tends to be _____ all of the other children in his class.
   (A) the same old to   (C) as old like
   (B) the same age than   (D) the same age as

12. Most foreign students don't like American coffee, and _____.
   (A) I don't too   (C) neither don't I
   (B) either don't I   (D) neither do I

13. We had hoped _____ the game, but the other team played very well.
   (A) State University to win
   (B) that State University win
   (C) that State University would win
   (D) State University's winning

14. This plant is _____ big that it should really be moved outside.
   (A) so   (C) such
   (B) too   (D) very

15. Unlike most Europeans, many Americans _____
bacon and eggs for breakfast every day.

- (A) used to eating
- (C) are used to eating
- (B) are used to eat
- (D) used to eat

Part B

Directions: Each question in Part B consists of a sentence in which four words or phrases are underlined. The four underlined parts of the sentence are marked (A), (B), (C), (D). You are to identify the *one* underlined word or phrase that would *not be accepted* in standard written English. Then, on your answer sheet, find the number of the question and mark your answer.

16. Whoever turned in the last test did not put their
              (A)   (B) (C)

name on the paper.
      (D)

17. The most common form of treatment it is mass
     (A)   (B)   (C)

inoculation and chlorination of water sources.
                            (D)

18. People with an exceptionally high intelligence quo-
               (A)

tient may not be the the best employees since
                   (B)

they become bored of their work unless the job
            (C)

is constantly changing.
          (D)

19. Neither the mathematics department nor the biology
                                                    (A)

department at State University requires that

the students must write a thesis in order
              (B)

to graduate with a master's degree.
    (C)   (D)

20. The oxygen content of Mars is not
       sufficient enough to support life as we
            (A)   (B)   (C)

know it.
   (D)

21. Students in the United States often support
                                          (A)

themselves by babysitting, working in restaur-
    (B)   (C)

ants, or they drive taxi cabs.
           (D)

22. Those of us who have a family history of heart dis-
                 (A)

ease should make yearly appointments with
        (B)   (C)

their doctors.
   (D)

23. Although federal support for basic research pro-
                              (A)

grams are much less than it was ten years ago,
      (B)   (C)   (D)

more funds are now available from the National
Science Foundation.

24. Living in New York, apartments cost more to rent
       (A)   (B)

than they do in other smaller cities.
   (C)   (D)

25. This new model not only saves time but also
    <u>(A)</u>

    energy by operating on two batteries instead of
    <u>(B)</u>   <u>(C)</u>   <u>(D)</u>

    four.

26. The government requires that a census be taken
                                              <u>(A)</u>

    every ten years   so   accurate   statistics
    <u>(B)</u>   <u>(C)</u>

    may be compiled.
    <u>(D)</u>

27. In 1975, according to the National Center for Health
               <u>(A)</u>

    Statistics, the average life expectancy for peo-

    ple born during that year is 72.4 years.
        <u>(B)</u> <u>(C)</u>   <u>(D)</u>

28. The flag is risen in the morning and taken down
                <u>(A)</u>   <u>(B)</u>

    at night by the boy scouts.
    <u>(C)</u>   <u>(D)</u>

29. When the silk worm gets through to lay its eggs, it
         <u>(A)</u>   <u>(B)</u> <u>(C)</u>

    dies.
    <u>(D)</u>

30. Frank Lloyd Wright has been acclaimed
                        <u>(A)</u>

    by colleagues as the greater of all modern ar-
    <u>(B)</u>   <u>(C)</u> <u>(D)</u>

    chitects.

31. Scientists had <u>previously</u> estimated that the Grand
　　　　　　　　　(A)

　　　Canyon in Arizona <u>is</u> ten million years old; but
　　　　　　　　　　　　　(B)

　　　now, <u>by using</u> a more modern dating method,
　　　　　　(C)

　　　they agree that the age is closer to
　　　<u>six million years</u>.
　　　　　(D)

32. There <u>have been</u> a tornado watch <u>issued</u> <u>for</u> Texas
　　　　　(A)　　　　　　　　　　　(B)　(C)

　　　County <u>until</u> eleven o'clock tonight.
　　　　　(D)

33. Professor Baker, with six of his graduate students,
　　　<u>are</u> attending a conference in Boston
　　　(A)

　　　<u>organized</u> <u>to compare</u> current business prac-
　　　　(B)　　　(C)

　　　tices in the United States with <u>those</u> of other
　　　　　　　　　　　　　　　　　(D)

　　　nations.

34. Jane Addams had <u>already</u> established Hull House
　　　　　　　　　　　(A)

　　　<u>in Chicago</u> and <u>began</u> her work in the Women's
　　　　(B)　　　　(C)

　　　Suffrage Movement when she was <u>awarded</u> the
　　　　　　　　　　　　　　　　　(D)

　　　Nobel Prize for peace.

35. If one had thought about the alternatives <u>you</u> would
　　　　　　　　　　　　　　　　　　　(A)

　　　not have <u>chosen</u> <u>such</u> a difficult topic for a
　　　　　　　(B)　　(C)

　　　<u>term paper</u>.
　　　　(D)

36. Although <u>jogging</u> is a good way to lose weight and
    (A)

    improve one's physical condition, <u>most</u> doctors
    (B)

    recommend that the potential jogger begin
    <u>in a correct manner</u> by <u>getting</u> a complete
        (C)   (D)

    check-up.

37. The flag of the <u>original first</u> colonies may or may not
    (A)

    <u>have been made</u> by <u>Betsy Ross</u>
        (B)   (C)

    <u>during the Revolution</u>.
        (D)

38. To the men <u>who</u> worked so <u>hard</u> on the project, the
            (A)   (B)

    news was <u>profound</u> <u>disappointing</u>.
            (C)   (D)

39. The Indians of the Southwestern United States
    <u>are</u> famous for their beautiful <u>art work,</u>
    (A)   (B)

    <u>especially</u> handmade jewelry cast from silver,
        (C)

    carved from stones, or <u>decorations</u> with beads,
                               (D)

    and feathers.

40. Because the solar tiles were very <u>secure fastened,</u>
                                        (A)

    only <u>a few</u> became <u>detached</u> when the Space
           (B)   (C)

    Shuttle reentered <u>the Earth's atmosphere</u>.
                           (D)

STOP. IF YOU HAVE FINISHED BEFORE TIME IS CALLED, CHECK YOUR
WORK ON THIS SECTION ONLY. DO NOT WORK ON ANY OTHER SECTION
OF THE TEST.

SECTION III: READING COMPREHENSION AND VOCABULARY

60 QUESTIONS
55 MINUTES

Part A

Directions: In each sentence of Part A, a word or phrase is underlined. Below each sentence are four other words or phrases. You are to choose the one word or phrase which would *best keep the meaning* of the original sentence if it were substituted for the underlined word.

1. Thomas Edison's office was always <u>disorganized</u> with books and papers.
   - (A) cluttered
   - (B) decorated
   - (C) sorted
   - (D) stacked

2. Sometimes items are put on sale because they have <u>imperfections</u> in them.
   - (A) defects
   - (B) mileage
   - (C) signatures
   - (D) installments

3. Historical records reveal that Jefferson <u>reiterated</u> his ideas about a meritocracy.
   - (A) furthered
   - (B) changed
   - (C) repeated
   - (D) published

4. Mail service will be <u>suspended</u> during the postal workers' strike.
   - (A) inspected
   - (B) delayed
   - (C) uninterrupted
   - (D) curtailed

5. In Benjamin Franklin's almanac, he warns against making <u>hasty</u> decisions.
   - (A) expensive
   - (B) unhealthy
   - (C) firm
   - (D) quick

6. A good student is eager to learn and does not need to be <u>warned</u> for being absent too much.
   - (A) admonished
   - (B) punished
   - (C) belittled
   - (D) spanked

7. An appendectomy is a <u>routine</u> operation.
   - (A) cheap
   - (B) small
   - (C) usual
   - (D) quick

8. Since research studies have shown a relationship between cancer and cigarette smoking, many people have cut down.
   (A) ceased smoking
   (B) become frightened
   (C) decreased the number of cigarettes
   (D) gotten sick

9. It is not a good business policy to buy sleazy materials.
   (A) few
   (B) cheap
   (C) used
   (D) old

10. Lifting the shoulders is a gesture that indicates lack of interest.
    (A) Napping
    (B) Shrugging
    (C) Sighing
    (D) Yawning

11. Some celestial bodies will leave luminous trails upon entering the earth's atmosphere.
    (A) junk
    (B) meteors
    (C) missiles
    (D) precipitation

12. In the play Virginia Wolfe a woman and her husband spend most of their time quarreling.
    (A) bickering
    (B) gossiping
    (C) teasing
    (D) chuckling

13. The author of a book, a musical composition, or an artistic work may choose to honor someone by putting his or her name in the front of it, thereby giving it.
    (A) consecrating
    (B) devoting
    (C) dedicating
    (D) pledging

14. Tiny Tim, a character in A Christmas Carol, was a happy little boy in spite of the disability that caused him to favor one leg.
    (A) limp
    (B) weep
    (C) rest
    (D) shout

15. Pipes may be painted to keep them from getting oxidized.
    (A) misplaced
    (B) soaked
    (C) rusty
    (D) frozen

16. <u>Interfering</u> with someone's mail is a serious crime in the U.S.
  (A) Assisting
  (B) Tampering
  (C) Gambling
  (D) Intimidating

17. <u>Finances</u> can consist of a combination of stocks, bonds, and properties.
  (A) Exceptions
  (B) Assets
  (C) Donations
  (D) Bequests

18. An understudy performs when the lead singer's voice becomes <u>hoarse</u>.
  (A) fatigued
  (B) thin
  (C) famous
  (D) rough

19. Rain <u>lessens</u> in the fall throughout most of the Appalachian Mountain region.
  (A) pours
  (B) accumulates
  (C) abates
  (D) evaporates

20. Several members of the royal family have been held <u>prisoner</u> in the Tower of London.
  (A) for protection
  (B) by request
  (C) captive
  (D) briefly

21. A marching band often performs during the <u>time</u> between the two halves of a football game.
  (A) interval
  (B) entertainment
  (C) yelling
  (D) interview

22. Athletes learn to <u>conceal</u> their disappointment when they lose.
  (A) ignore
  (B) regret
  (C) accept
  (D) disguise

23. Although monkeys occasionally <u>menace</u> their enemies, they are usually not dangerous unless they are provoked.
  (A) pursue
  (B) consume
  (C) threaten
  (D) kill

24. Many of the first histories of the New World were written by monks and <u>published</u> by the Catholic Church.
  (A) put away
  (B) brought out
  (C) approved of
  (D) thrown out

25. Valium is a strong drug that can cause a driver to <u>sleep</u> at the wheel.

    (A) dream   (C) doze

    (B) sneeze   (D) snore

26. Milk is <u>purified</u> by heating it at 60°C. for thirty minutes.

    (A) cleansed   (C) mixed

    (B) stored   (D) packaged

27. The box fell off his desk and hit the floor with a <u>thump</u>.

    (A) a dull noise   (C) a musical sound

    (B) a very small sound (D) a repeated noise

28. Flu shots are given every fall as a <u>precaution</u> against an epidemic the following winter.

    (A) required treatment   (C) free service

    (B) preventive measure   (D) new cure

29. When a hurricane is <u>about to occur</u>, the National Weather Bureau issues a warning.

    (A) adjacent   (C) gigantic

    (B) perilous   (D) imminent

30. Unless the population growth stabilizes, environmentalists predict a worldwide <u>starvation</u> by the year 2000 A.D.

    (A) famine   (C) rebellion

    (B) flood   (D) disease

Part B

Directions: In Part B, you will be given a variety of reading material (single sentences, paragraphs, advertisements, and the like) followed by questions about the meaning of the material. You are to choose the *one* best answer, (A), (B), (C), or (D), to each question. Then, on your answer sheet, find the number of the problem and mark your answer. Answer all questions following a passage on the basis of what is *stated* or *implied* in that passage.

Questions 31–35 refer to the following passage:

A geyser is the result of underground water under the combined conditions of high temperatures and increased pressure beneath the surface of the earth. Since temperature rises approximately one degree F. for every sixty feet under the earth's surface, and pressure increases with depth, water that seeps down in cracks and fissures until it reaches very hot rocks in the earth's interior becomes heated to a temperature in excess of 290 degrees F. Because of the greater pressure, it shoots out of the surface in the form of steam and hot water. The result is a geyser.

For the most part, geysers are located in three regions of the world: New Zealand, Iceland, and the Yellowstone National Park area of the United States. The most famous geyser in the world is Old Faithful in Yellowstone Park. Old Faithful erupts almost every hour, rising to a height of 125 to 170 feet and expelling more than ten thousand gallons during each eruption.

31. In order for a geyser to erupt
    (A) hot rocks must rise to the surface of the earth
    (B) water must flow underground
    (C) it must be a warm day
    (D) the earth must not be rugged or broken
32. Old Faithful is located in
    (A) New Zealand
    (B) Iceland
    (C) the United States
    (D) England
33. Old Faithful erupts
    (A) every 10 minutes
    (B) every 60 minutes
    (C) every 125 minutes
    (D) every 170 minutes
34. A geyser is
    (A) hot water and steam
    (B) cracks and fissures
    (C) hot rocks
    (D) great pressure

35. As depth increases
  (A) pressure increases but temperature does not
  (B) temperature increases but pressure does not
  (C) both pressure and temperature increase
  (D) neither pressure nor temperature increases

Questions 36–37 refer to the following sentence:

  Stamp collecting, or to call it by its correct name, philately, has been an increasingly popular hobby from as early as 1854.

36. What is another name for stamp collecting?
  (A) popular
  (B) philately
  (C) hobby
  (D) increasingly

37. In 1854, stamp collecting was _____.
  (A) more popular than it is today
  (B) as popular as it is today
  (C) not enjoyed
  (D) just beginning to become popular

Questions 38–40 refer to the following passage:

  The influenza virus is a single molecule composed of millions of individual atoms. While bacteria can be considered as a type of plant, secreting poisonous substances into the body of the organism they attack, viruses, like the influenza virus, are living organisms themselves. We may consider them as regular chemical molecules since they have strictly defined atomic structure; but on the other hand, we must also consider them as being alive since they are able to multiply in unlimited quantities.

38. According to this passage, bacteria are
  (A) poisons
  (B) very small
  (C) larger than viruses
  (D) plants

39. The writer says that viruses are alive because they
    (A) have a complex atomic structure
    (B) move
    (C) multiply
    (D) need warmth and light
40. The atomic structure of viruses
    (A) is variable
    (B) is strictly defined
    (C) cannot be analyzed chemically
    (D) is more complex than that of bacteria

Questions 41–45 refer to the following passage:

A green I–538 form is used by international students in order to obtain permission from the Immigration and Naturalization Service to transfer from one university to another in the United States. If you are planning to transfer, remember that you must obtain the permission before leaving the university where you are currently studying. You must complete the form I–538, have it signed by the foreign student advisor, and submit it to the District Office of the Immigration and Naturalization Service together with the form I–20 from your new school and the small, white form I–94 that was affixed to your passport when you entered the country.

Submitting the signed I–538 and other documents does not insure permission to transfer. Only an official of Immigration can decide each case. Students who have not completed one term of study at the school that issued them their first I–20 are not advised to file for permission to transfer until they have completed one term.

41. A transfer form is called an
    (A) I–20   (C) I–538
    (B) I–94   (D) I–520

42. If you want to transfer it is a good idea to
   - (A) travel to the new university immediately so that the foreign student advisor can help you
   - (B) study at the university where you have permission until you receive a new permission from Immigration
   - (C) sign an I–538 form and leave it at your current university before traveling to the new university
   - (D) leave the country so that you can enter on another I–20 from the new university

43. In order for you to transfer, permission must be granted by an official at the
   - (A) foreign student advisor's office
   - (B) new university
   - (C) Immigration office
   - (D) passport office

44. The transfer form must be signed by the
   - (A) foreign student advisor at the new school
   - (B) foreign student advisor at the current school
   - (C) student
   - (D) Immigration officer

45. This passage is mainly about
   - (A) the Immigration and Naturalization Service
   - (B) how to get a passport
   - (C) how to obtain permission to transfer from one university to another
   - (D) studying in the United States

Questions 46–47 refer to the following sentence:

In modern urban centers, the unburned hydrocarbons, nitrogen oxides and carbon monoxides in automotive exhaust are the greatest source of photochemical air pollution, or smog.

46. In order to lessen smog, which of the following should be reduced?
   (A) the number of cameras
   (B) the number of factories
   (C) the number of cars
   (D) the number of fires

47. Which of the following words or phrases has the same meaning as smog?
   (A) urban centers
   (B) automotive exhaust
   (C) photochemical air pollution
   (D) hydrocarbons

Questions 48–50 refer to the following passage:

Although most universities in the United States are on a semester system which offers classes in the fall and spring, some schools observe a quarter system comprised of fall, winter, spring, and summer quarters. The academic year, September to June, is divided into three quarters of eleven weeks each beginning in September, January, and March; the summer quarter, June to August, is composed of shorter sessions of varying length. Students may take advantage of the opportunity to study year around by enrolling in all four quarters. Most students begin their programs in the fall quarter, but they may enter at the beginning of any of the other quarters.

48. The academic year is
   (A) September to August
   (B) June to August
   (C) August to June
   (D) September to June

49. A semester system
   (A) has eleven-week sessions
   (B) is not very popular in the United States
   (C) gives students the opportunity to study year around
   (D) has two major sessions a year

50. Which of the following would be the best title for this passage?
   (A)   Universities in The United States
   (B)   The Academic Year
   (C)   The Quarter System
   (D)   The Semester System

Questions 51–55 refer to the following instructions:

Adults .... 2 tablespoonfuls
Children: according to age:
10–14 years .... 4 teaspoonfuls
 6–10 years .... 2 teaspoonfuls
 3–6   years .... 1 teaspoonful
Repeat above dosage every ½ hour to
1 hour if needed until 8 doses are taken.
If relief does not occur within two days,
consult a physician.
    SHAKE WELL BEFORE USING

51. According to the instructions, what should you do before taking this medication?
   (A)   Mix it   (C)   Add water to it
   (B)   Heat it   (D)   See a doctor

52. For whom would a dosage of two teaspoonfuls be recommended?
   (A)   An adult
   (B)   A 10-to-14-year-old child
   (C)   A 6-to-10-year-old child
   (D)   A 3-to-6-year-old child

53. What is the maximum amount of medication that should be taken by an adult in a four-hour period?
   (A)   Two doses   (C)   Six doses
   (B)   Four doses   (D)   Eight doses

54. How are children's dosages determined?
   (A)   By the weight of the child
   (B)   By the age of the child
   (C)   By the time of day
   (D)   By consulting a physician

55. Most likely, this medication is _____.
- (A) a pill
- (B) an injection
- (C) a lozenge
- (D) a liquid

Questions 56–60. For each of these questions, choose the answer that is closest in meaning to the original sentence. Note that several of the choices may be factually correct, but you should choose the one that is the closest restatement of the given sentence.

56. It usually takes about four weeks to process a social security card after the application and necessary evidence of age, identity and citizenship have been received at the local social security office.
- (A) Before submitting evidence of age, identity and citizenship to the social security office, it is necessary to have a card.
- (B) Four weeks before one needs a social security card, he should submit evidence of age, identity and citizenship, along with an application to the local social security office.
- (C) One must submit evidence of age, identity and citizenship four weeks after the social security office processes your card.
- (D) The local social security office will provide evidence of age, identity and citizenship four weeks after one submits an application.

57. Mobil Oil Corporation points out that if a driver reduces his speed from 70 to 50 miles per hour, the car driven will average 25 percent more mileage per gallon.
    - (A) More gasoline is needed in order to drive slowly according to Mobil Oil Corporation.
    - (B) Mobil Oil Corporation reports that a reduction in speed will result in an increase in the consumption of gasoline.
    - (C) According to Mobil Oil Corporation, an increase in speed causes an increase in mileage per gallon of gasoline.
    - (D) Less gasoline is consumed at slower speeds according to Mobil Oil Corporation.

58. Despite the great difference in size, shape, and function, all cells have the same 46 chromosomes.
    - (A) All cells are the same because the 46 chromosomes govern size, shape and function.
    - (B) Differences in size, shape and function are not very great because all cells have the same 46 chromosomes.
    - (C) The size, shape and function of cells are the same, but the 46 chromosomes are different.
    - (D) Although the 46 chromosomes are the same in all cells, there are differences in the size, shape, and function.

59. Unless the trend reverses, low-priced pocket calculators will have replaced the slide rule completely within the next few years.
    - (A) Slide rules will have been replaced by low-priced pocket calculators soon if the trend continues.
    - (B) More people will be using slide rules than pocket calculators even though they are more expensive, unless the trend reverses.
    - (C) Because they are low-priced, pocket calculators will replace slide rules in the next few years.
    - (D) The trend is for slide rules to be used in spite of the low prices of pocket calculators.

60. No one except the graduate assistant understood the results of the experiments.
- (A) All of the graduate assistants understood the experiments.
- (B) The experiments were not understood by any of them.
- (C) Only the graduate assistant understood the experiments.
- (D) All but one of the graduate assistants understood the experiments.

STOP. IF YOU HAVE FINISHED BEFORE TIME IS CALLED, CHECK YOUR WORK ON THIS SECTION ONLY. DO NOT WORK ON ANY OTHER SECTION OF THE TEST.

Answer Key—Model Test 1

Section I: Listening Comprehension

1. (C)	11. (B)	21. (B)	31. (C)	41. (C)
2. (D)	12. (C)	22. (C)	32. (C)	42. (B)
3. (A)	13. (C)	23. (D)	33. (A)	43. (D)
4. (D)	14. (C)	24. (B)	34. (C)	44. (C)
5. (B)	15. (B)	25. (B)	35. (C)	45. (B)
6. (D)	16. (A)	26. (C)	36. (A)	46. (C)
7. (D)	17. (D)	27. (A)	37. (C)	47. (A)
8. (A)	18. (C)	28. (C)	38. (C)	48. (B)
9. (B)	19. (C)	29. (C)	39. (B)	49. (B)
10. (A)	20. (B)	30. (B)	40. (C)	50. (D)

Section II: Structure and Written Expression

1. (B)	9. (C)	17. (C)	25. (B)	33. (A)
2. (A)	10. (D)	18. (C)	26. (C)	34. (C)
3. (D)	11. (D)	19. (B)	27. (D)	35. (A)
4. (B)	12. (D)	20. (A)	28. (A)	36. (C)
5. (B)	13. (C)	21. (D)	29. (B)	37. (A)
6. (D)	14. (A)	22. (D)	30. (D)	38. (D)
7. (C)	15. (C)	23. (B)	31. (B)	39. (D)
8. (A)	16. (C)	24. (A)	32. (A)	40. (A)

Section III: Reading Comprehension and Vocabulary

1. (A)	13. (C)	25. (C)	37. (D)	49. (D)
2. (A)	14. (A)	26. (A)	38. (D)	50. (C)
3. (C)	15. (C)	27. (A)	39. (C)	51. (A)
4. (D)	16. (B)	28. (B)	40. (B)	52. (C)
5. (D)	17. (B)	29. (D)	41. (C)	53. (D)
6. (A)	18. (D)	30. (A)	42. (B)	54. (B)
7. (C)	19. (C)	31. (B)	43. (C)	55. (D)
8. (C)	20. (C)	32. (C)	44. (B)	56. (B)
9. (B)	21. (A)	33. (B)	45. (C)	57. (D)
10. (B)	22. (D)	34. (A)	46. (C)	58. (D)
11. (B)	23. (C)	35. (C)	47. (C)	59. (A)
12. (A)	24. (B)	36. (B)	48. (D)	60. (C)

Transcript for the Listening Comprehension Test— Model Test 1

In this section of the test, you will have an opportunity to demonstrate your ability to understand spoken English. It is in three parts, and there are special directions for each part. [For the directions to each part, see the corresponding portion in the test. The listening comprehension section is on the cassette included with this test book.]

Part A

Directions: For the directions to this part, see page 111.

(*Note:* The reader should say the question number preceding each test question. For example, the reader should say, "Question number one. This year State University . . .")

1. This year State University will celebrate its fiftieth anniversary as a state institution.

(*Note:* There should be a 15-second pause after each test question in this section.)

2. The weather was supposed to be nice today, but it rained most of the afternoon.

3. Mrs. Jones told me that her neighbors were moving to Florida.

4. Even though I would rather not go, I must be present at the funeral.

5. Tom wouldn't have told her about it if he had known that the party was supposed to be a surprise.

6. John planned to buy a used car for two thousand dollars because a new one would have cost him twice that much.

7. John is an A student, but this term he got a C in French.

8. If you need assistance, please stay on the line until an operator answers.

9. Although Miss Smith has had less teaching experience than the other members of the staff, she is one of the best instructors.

10. I have never felt better than I do now.

11. The paper boy is here at five o'clock every day, but today he is a little late.

12. We had enough chairs for thirty people, but three times that many showed up.

13. Steve is better looking, but his brother is more popular with the girls.

14. Five couples belong to the club.

15. Mary had to save for two years in order to have enough money for her vacation to Europe.

16. Since we got stuck in traffic for three hours, we didn't arrive until four o'clock.

17. If I could sew as well as Jane I would make all of my own clothes too.

18. We started to go to the basketball game, but we ended up at the disco instead.

19. Some people think that pets should live in the house, but as far as I am concerned, they belong outside.

20. She would not apologize even though she was sorry.

Part B

Directions: For the directions to this part, see page 114.

(*Note:* In this section, three readers are required: one man, one woman, and one narrator—either man or woman. The narrator reads the question number and the question following the dialogue.)

21. *Man:*   Gas is sixty cents now. I couldn't be-
                  lieve it when I drove into the service
                  station.

     Woman: I know. It has gone up a nickel a gallon
                  in the past month alone. It will prob-
                  ably be sixty-five cents by next month.

     Third Voice: How much was the price of gasoline
                  last month?

(*Note:* There should be a 15-second pause after each test
question in this section.)

22. *Man:*   Let me help you with that, Mrs. Wilson.

     Woman: Well thank you, Jim. Why don't you get
                  the hoe and loosen the soil in that
                  flower bed for me?

     Third Voice: Where did the conversation most
                  probably take place?

23. *Man:*   Jane, I would like to introduce you to
                  my sister, Ellen.

     Woman: Glad to meet you, Ellen. Bob tells me
                  that you are interested in African art
                  too. In fact, he says that you plan to
                  spend the summer in Zimbabwe.

     Third Voice: What do the girls have in common?

24. *Man:*   What are you going to do this week-
                  end? Maybe we can play some tennis.

     Woman: Don't tempt me. I have to study for my
                  qualifying examinations. I take them
                  on Monday.

     Third Voice: Why didn't the woman agree to play
                  tennis?

25. *Woman:*   Where is the best place to buy cakes?

     Man: Well, The Dutch Oven is the best place,
                  but it is closed right now. Why don't
                  you try Mamma's Bake Shop on Wells
                  Street?

     Third Voice: Why will the woman go to the bakery
                  on Wells Street?

26. *Woman:* How do you like your new job, Bill?

Man: Fine. This week I have been reading the financial reports and studying the books. Next week I will probably start to handle some of the accounts.

Third Voice: What does the man do for a living?

27. *Man:* That is $3.25 on the meter, and a dollar extra for the suitcases.

Woman: Okay. Here is five dollars. Keep the change.

Third Voice: How much was the driver's tip?

28. *Man:* Have you talked to Ali lately? I thought that he was studying at the American Language Institute, but yesterday I saw him going into the chemistry lab in the engineering building.

Woman: That is not surprising. Ali is a part-time student this term. He is taking three classes at the Institute and one class at the university.

Third Voice: What do we learn about Ali?

29. *Man:* Hello, Miss Evans? This is Paul Thompson. I would like to talk with my wife, please.

Woman: Oh, Paul. You just missed her. She left the office a few minutes early so she could stop by the bank on her way home.

Third Voice: Where is Mrs. Thompson?

30. *Man:* I would like to take an X-ray, Mrs. Johnson. I can't be sure, but I think you have a small cavity starting in one of your back molars, and if so, I want to get it filled before it begins to give you problems.

Woman: I have been so careful about eating too many sweets too. I don't know why my teeth get so many cavities.

Third Voice:	What is the probable relationship between the two speakers?

31. *Woman:* Just give me a haircut today. It won't do any good to set it because I am going swimming at Lake Florida this afternoon anyway.

Man: Okay. But you will want to look nice on the way there. Why don't I put a few rollers in the top?

Third Voice: What do we learn from this conversation?

32. *Man:* I would like to see Mr. Adams, please.

Woman: Mr. Adams is not here anymore. Mrs. Jones is the foreign student advisor now.

Third Voice: What do we learn from this conversation?

33. *Man:* Hi, Mary. Did you get a letter from your family?

Woman: Not today. I just wrote them day before yesterday so I am not really expecting to hear from them until next week. This is a telephone bill.

Third Voice: What did the woman say about a letter?

34. *Man:* I am sorry, Miss. Flight 622 has already departed.

Woman: Oh. All right. Can you please tell me where I can find a telephone?

Third Voice: What does the woman want to know?

35. *Man:* Have you bought your books yet?

Woman: I got my English book, but the math and history books were sold out. We don't have a book for my music course.

Third Voice: Which book has the woman bought?

Part C

Directions: For the directions to this part, see page 116.

MINI-TALK ONE

There have been a number of important American novelists in this century, but F. Scott Fitzgerald is one of the more interesting ones. Born in 1896, educated at Princeton, his novels describe the post-war American society, very much caught up in the rhythms of jazz.

In 1920, the same year that he published his first book, *This Side of Paradise*, he married Zelda Sayre, also a writer. His most famous book, *The Great Gatsby*, appeared in 1925.

Fitzgerald had a great natural talent, but he was a compulsive drinker. A brilliant success in his youth, he never made the adjustments necessary to a maturing writer in a changing world. His later novels, *All the Sad Young Men*, *Tender is the Night*, and *The Last Tycoon*, were less successful, so that when he died in 1940 his books were out of print and he had been almost forgotten.

His reputation now is far greater than it was in his lifetime, especially since the film version of his novel, *The Great Gatsby*, was released.

36. According to the lecturer, what do we know about the novels written by F. Scott Fitzgerald?

(*Note:* There should be a 15-second pause after each test question in this section.)

37. When did Fitzgerald achieve his greatest success?

38. Which of Fitzgerald's novels has been made into a movie?

39. What does the lecturer tell us about Fitzgerald's personality?

40. When did Fitzgerald publish his novel, *The Great Gatsby?*

MINI-TALK TWO

Toledo Express Airport has asked us to announce that all incoming and outgoing commercial flights have been canceled this evening due to adverse weather conditions at Toledo and neighboring airports. Detroit Metro Airport is closed. Chicago O'Hare Airport is closed.

All en-route traffic for these airports has been diverted to Port Columbus International Airport and the Greater Cincinnati Airport.

A traveler's advisory is in effect and a winter storm watch has been issued for North Central Ohio and Southern Michigan, with an expected accumulation of four inches of snow and near blizzard conditions overnight.

Passengers booked on flights tomorrow are advised to call the airport in order to confirm their departures.

For further information as we receive it, stay tuned to WLQR 101 FM on your radio dial.

41. Which of the area airports is open?

42. What should passengers do if they hold tickets for flights tomorrow?

43. What kind of adverse weather conditions have caused the airports to close?

MINI-TALK THREE

Man: This is it. I know that it is smaller than you wanted, but it is one of the nicest apartments in the building.

Woman: Does it have three bedrooms?

Man: No. There are two. The master bedroom is quite spacious though. Maybe you could let the children share the larger room, and you and your husband could use the smaller one.

Woman:	I suppose that I could do that.
Man:	A three-bedroom apartment will be difficult to find.
Woman:	Yes, I know. Believe me, I have been looking for over a week. The few three-bedroom apartments that I have found are either extremely expensive or the owner won't allow children as tenants.
Man:	Well, the owner allows two children in this apartment complex.
Woman:	Aren't you the owner?
Man:	No. I am the manager. I live here, too, on the first floor of this building.
Woman:	Oh. That's nice. Then if anything gets broken . . .
Man:	Just leave a note on my door.
Woman:	You said that the rent would be $350 a month. Does that include any of the utilities?
Man:	Yes. It includes gas. Your furnace and stove are gas, so, as you can imagine, your other utilities, electric and water, are quite inexpensive.
Woman:	This sounds better and better. But before I sign a lease I would like for my husband to see it.
Man:	Why not stop by with him this evening?
Woman:	How late are you open? He doesn't get off work until five.
Man:	Come by at six. I will still be in the office. I am sure that you are eager to move from the hotel, and if we get the paper work out of the way tonight, you can move in tomorrow.
Woman:	Oh, that would be wonderful.

44. Who is the man in this conversation?
45. Where is the woman living now?
46. Why didn't the woman sign a lease?

MINI-TALK FOUR

Health food is a general term applied to all kinds of foods that are considered more healthful than the types of foods widely sold in supermarkets. For example, whole grains, dried beans, and corn oil are health foods. A narrower classification of health food is natural food. This term is used to distinguish between types of the same food. Raw honey is a natural sweetener, whereas refined sugar is not. Fresh fruit is a natural food, but canned fruit, with sugars and other additives, is not. The most precise term of all and the narrowest classification within health foods is organic food, used to describe food that has been grown on a particular kind of farm. Fruits and vegetables that are grown in gardens that are treated only with organic fertilizers, that are not sprayed with poisonous insecticides, and that are not refined after harvest, are organic foods. Meats, fish, dairy and poultry products from animals that are fed only organically grown feed and that are not injected with hormones are organic foods.

In choosing the type of food you eat, then, you have basically two choices: inorganic, processed foods, or organic, unprocessed foods. A wise decision should include investigation of the allegations that processed foods contain chemicals, some of which are proven to be toxic, and that vitamin content is greatly reduced in processed foods.

Bread is typically used by health food advocates as an example of a processed food. First, the seeds from which the grain is grown are treated with bichloride of mercury, an extremely toxic poison. Later, the grain is sprayed with a number of very toxic insecticides and pesticides. After the grain has been made into flour, it is bleached with nitrogen trichloride or chlorine dioxide, both toxic. Next, a dough conditioner, usually ammonium chloride, is added along with a softener, polyoxyethylene. The conditioner and softener are poisons, and in fact, the softener has sickened and killed experimental animals.

A very toxic antioxidant is now added, along with coal tar, a butter-like yellow dye. Finally calcium propionate, an anti-fungal compound, is added to keep the bread from getting moldy.

Other foods from the supermarket would show a similar pattern of processing and preserving. You see, we buy our food on the basis of smell, color, and texture, instead of vitamin content, and manufacturers give us what we want—even if it is poisonous.

The alternative? Eat health foods, preferably the organic variety.

47. What was the main idea of this talk?
48. Which term is used to distinguish between types of the same food?
49. What did all of the additives in bread have in common?
50. What happens to food when it is processed?

Answer Sheet—Model Test 2

Section I: Listening Comprehension

1. Ⓐ Ⓑ Ⓒ Ⓓ
2. Ⓐ Ⓑ Ⓒ Ⓓ
3. Ⓐ Ⓑ Ⓒ Ⓓ
4. Ⓐ Ⓑ Ⓒ Ⓓ
5. Ⓐ Ⓑ Ⓒ Ⓓ
6. Ⓐ Ⓑ Ⓒ Ⓓ
7. Ⓐ Ⓑ Ⓒ Ⓓ
8. Ⓐ Ⓑ Ⓒ Ⓓ
9. Ⓐ Ⓑ Ⓒ Ⓓ
10. Ⓐ Ⓑ Ⓒ Ⓓ
11. Ⓐ Ⓑ Ⓒ Ⓓ
12. Ⓐ Ⓑ Ⓒ Ⓓ
13. Ⓐ Ⓑ Ⓒ Ⓓ
14. Ⓐ Ⓑ Ⓒ Ⓓ
15. Ⓐ Ⓑ Ⓒ Ⓓ
16. Ⓐ Ⓑ Ⓒ Ⓓ
17. Ⓐ Ⓑ Ⓒ Ⓓ
18. Ⓐ Ⓑ Ⓒ Ⓓ
19. Ⓐ Ⓑ Ⓒ Ⓓ
20. Ⓐ Ⓑ Ⓒ Ⓓ
21. Ⓐ Ⓑ Ⓒ Ⓓ
22. Ⓐ Ⓑ Ⓒ Ⓓ
23. Ⓐ Ⓑ Ⓒ Ⓓ
24. Ⓐ Ⓑ Ⓒ Ⓓ
25. Ⓐ Ⓑ Ⓒ Ⓓ
26. Ⓐ Ⓑ Ⓒ Ⓓ
27. Ⓐ Ⓑ Ⓒ Ⓓ
28. Ⓐ Ⓑ Ⓒ Ⓓ
29. Ⓐ Ⓑ Ⓒ Ⓓ
30. Ⓐ Ⓑ Ⓒ Ⓓ
31. Ⓐ Ⓑ Ⓒ Ⓓ
32. Ⓐ Ⓑ Ⓒ Ⓓ
33. Ⓐ Ⓑ Ⓒ Ⓓ
34. Ⓐ Ⓑ Ⓒ Ⓓ
35. Ⓐ Ⓑ Ⓒ Ⓓ
36. Ⓐ Ⓑ Ⓒ Ⓓ
37. Ⓐ Ⓑ Ⓒ Ⓓ
38. Ⓐ Ⓑ Ⓒ Ⓓ
39. Ⓐ Ⓑ Ⓒ Ⓓ
40. Ⓐ Ⓑ Ⓒ Ⓓ
41. Ⓐ Ⓑ Ⓒ Ⓓ
42. Ⓐ Ⓑ Ⓒ Ⓓ
43. Ⓐ Ⓑ Ⓒ Ⓓ
44. Ⓐ Ⓑ Ⓒ Ⓓ
45. Ⓐ Ⓑ Ⓒ Ⓓ
46. Ⓐ Ⓑ Ⓒ Ⓓ
47. Ⓐ Ⓑ Ⓒ Ⓓ
48. Ⓐ Ⓑ Ⓒ Ⓓ
49. Ⓐ Ⓑ Ⓒ Ⓓ
50. Ⓐ Ⓑ Ⓒ Ⓓ

Section II: Structure and Written Expression

1. Ⓐ Ⓑ Ⓒ Ⓓ	21. Ⓐ Ⓑ Ⓒ Ⓓ
2. Ⓐ Ⓑ Ⓒ Ⓓ	22. Ⓐ Ⓑ Ⓒ Ⓓ
3. Ⓐ Ⓑ Ⓒ Ⓓ	23. Ⓐ Ⓑ Ⓒ Ⓓ
4. Ⓐ Ⓑ Ⓒ Ⓓ	24. Ⓐ Ⓑ Ⓒ Ⓓ
5. Ⓐ Ⓑ Ⓒ Ⓓ	25. Ⓐ Ⓑ Ⓒ Ⓓ
6. Ⓐ Ⓑ Ⓒ Ⓓ	26. Ⓐ Ⓑ Ⓒ Ⓓ
7. Ⓐ Ⓑ Ⓒ Ⓓ	27. Ⓐ Ⓑ Ⓒ Ⓓ
8. Ⓐ Ⓑ Ⓒ Ⓓ	28. Ⓐ Ⓑ Ⓒ Ⓓ
9. Ⓐ Ⓑ Ⓒ Ⓓ	29. Ⓐ Ⓑ Ⓒ Ⓓ
10. Ⓐ Ⓑ Ⓒ Ⓓ	30. Ⓐ Ⓑ Ⓒ Ⓓ
11. Ⓐ Ⓑ Ⓒ Ⓓ	31. Ⓐ Ⓑ Ⓒ Ⓓ
12. Ⓐ Ⓑ Ⓒ Ⓓ	32. Ⓐ Ⓑ Ⓒ Ⓓ
13. Ⓐ Ⓑ Ⓒ Ⓓ	33. Ⓐ Ⓑ Ⓒ Ⓓ
14. Ⓐ Ⓑ Ⓒ Ⓓ	34. Ⓐ Ⓑ Ⓒ Ⓓ
15. Ⓐ Ⓑ Ⓒ Ⓓ	35. Ⓐ Ⓑ Ⓒ Ⓓ
16. Ⓐ Ⓑ Ⓒ Ⓓ	36. Ⓐ Ⓑ Ⓒ Ⓓ
17. Ⓐ Ⓑ Ⓒ Ⓓ	37. Ⓐ Ⓑ Ⓒ Ⓓ
18. Ⓐ Ⓑ Ⓒ Ⓓ	38. Ⓐ Ⓑ Ⓒ Ⓓ
19. Ⓐ Ⓑ Ⓒ Ⓓ	39. Ⓐ Ⓑ Ⓒ Ⓓ
20. Ⓐ Ⓑ Ⓒ Ⓓ	40. Ⓐ Ⓑ Ⓒ Ⓓ

Section III: Reading Comprehension and Vocabulary

1. Ⓐ Ⓑ Ⓒ Ⓓ
2. Ⓐ Ⓑ Ⓒ Ⓓ
3. Ⓐ Ⓑ Ⓒ Ⓓ
4. Ⓐ Ⓑ Ⓒ Ⓓ
5. Ⓐ Ⓑ Ⓒ Ⓓ
6. Ⓐ Ⓑ Ⓒ Ⓓ
7. Ⓐ Ⓑ Ⓒ Ⓓ
8. Ⓐ Ⓑ Ⓒ Ⓓ
9. Ⓐ Ⓑ Ⓒ Ⓓ
10. Ⓐ Ⓑ Ⓒ Ⓓ
11. Ⓐ Ⓑ Ⓒ Ⓓ
12. Ⓐ Ⓑ Ⓒ Ⓓ
13. Ⓐ Ⓑ Ⓒ Ⓓ
14. Ⓐ Ⓑ Ⓒ Ⓓ
15. Ⓐ Ⓑ Ⓒ Ⓓ
16. Ⓐ Ⓑ Ⓒ Ⓓ
17. Ⓐ Ⓑ Ⓒ Ⓓ
18. Ⓐ Ⓑ Ⓒ Ⓓ
19. Ⓐ Ⓑ Ⓒ Ⓓ
20. Ⓐ Ⓑ Ⓒ Ⓓ
21. Ⓐ Ⓑ Ⓒ Ⓓ
22. Ⓐ Ⓑ Ⓒ Ⓓ
23. Ⓐ Ⓑ Ⓒ Ⓓ
24. Ⓐ Ⓑ Ⓒ Ⓓ
25. Ⓐ Ⓑ Ⓒ Ⓓ
26. Ⓐ Ⓑ Ⓒ Ⓓ
27. Ⓐ Ⓑ Ⓒ Ⓓ
28. Ⓐ Ⓑ Ⓒ Ⓓ
29. Ⓐ Ⓑ Ⓒ Ⓓ
30. Ⓐ Ⓑ Ⓒ Ⓓ

31. Ⓐ Ⓑ Ⓒ Ⓓ
32. Ⓐ Ⓑ Ⓒ Ⓓ
33. Ⓐ Ⓑ Ⓒ Ⓓ
34. Ⓐ Ⓑ Ⓒ Ⓓ
35. Ⓐ Ⓑ Ⓒ Ⓓ
36. Ⓐ Ⓑ Ⓒ Ⓓ
37. Ⓐ Ⓑ Ⓒ Ⓓ
38. Ⓐ Ⓑ Ⓒ Ⓓ
39. Ⓐ Ⓑ Ⓒ Ⓓ
40. Ⓐ Ⓑ Ⓒ Ⓓ
41. Ⓐ Ⓑ Ⓒ Ⓓ
42. Ⓐ Ⓑ Ⓒ Ⓓ
43. Ⓐ Ⓑ Ⓒ Ⓓ
44. Ⓐ Ⓑ Ⓒ Ⓓ
45. Ⓐ Ⓑ Ⓒ Ⓓ
46. Ⓐ Ⓑ Ⓒ Ⓓ
47. Ⓐ Ⓑ Ⓒ Ⓓ
48. Ⓐ Ⓑ Ⓒ Ⓓ
49. Ⓐ Ⓑ Ⓒ Ⓓ
50. Ⓐ Ⓑ Ⓒ Ⓓ
51. Ⓐ Ⓑ Ⓒ Ⓓ
52. Ⓐ Ⓑ Ⓒ Ⓓ
53. Ⓐ Ⓑ Ⓒ Ⓓ
54. Ⓐ Ⓑ Ⓒ Ⓓ
55. Ⓐ Ⓑ Ⓒ Ⓓ
56. Ⓐ Ⓑ Ⓒ Ⓓ
57. Ⓐ Ⓑ Ⓒ Ⓓ
58. Ⓐ Ⓑ Ⓒ Ⓓ
59. Ⓐ Ⓑ Ⓒ Ⓓ
60. Ⓐ Ⓑ Ⓒ Ⓓ

Model Test 2

The Test

SECTION I: LISTENING COMPREHENSION

In this section of the test, you will have an opportunity to demonstrate your ability to understand spoken English. It is in three parts, and there are special directions for each part.

Note: The transcript for the Listening Comprehension Section can be found on page 184.

Part A

Directions: For each problem in Part A, you will hear a short statement. The statements will be *spoken* just one time. They will not be written out for you, and you must listen carefully in order to understand what the speaker says.

When you hear a statement, read the four sentences in your test book and decide which one is closest in meaning to the statement you have heard. Then, on your answer sheet, find the number of the problem and mark your answer.

1. (A) Bob did not wear a ring because he was single.
   (B) Bob wore a ring because he was married.
   (C) Bob was single, but he wore a ring.
   (D) Bob was married, but he did not wear a ring.

2. (A) Mrs. Black thinks that it might rain.
   (B) Mrs. Black will go with her son.
   (C) It is very sunny.
   (D) Mrs. Black thinks that her son should stay home.

3. (A) You should leave at eight-thirty.
   (B) The play starts at eight-thirty.
   (C) The play starts at seven-thirty.
   (D) You should leave at eight o'clock.

4. (A) He would like to have a smaller car.
   (B) He would like to trade his small car.
   (C) He will trade his car for a bigger one.
   (D) He will not trade his car.

5. (A) Ms. Kent is a teacher.
   (B) Ms. Kent is a doctor.
   (C) Ms. Kent is a businesswoman.
   (D) Ms. Kent is a lawyer.

6. (A) Jim was paying attention, but he did not hear the question.
   (B) Jim was not paying attention and he did not hear the question.
   (C) Jim was not paying attention, but he heard the question.
   (D) Jim was paying attention and he heard the question.

7. (A) Joe was at the dormitory.
   (B) Joe was at home.
   (C) Joe was in the hospital.
   (D) Joe was the head resident.

8. (A) Twenty people came.
   (B) Thirty people came.
   (C) Forty people came.
   (D) Only one person came.

9. (A) It was a perfect paper.
   (B) The word was spelled perfectly.
   (C) The paper had one mistake.
   (D) The teacher did not accept the paper.

10. (A) The concert began at seven-forty-five.
    (B) The concert began at eight o'clock.
    (C) The concert began at eight-fifteen.
    (D) The concert began at eight-forty-five.

11. (A) Sally likes to talk on the telephone with her friends.
    (B) Sally does not like to talk on the telephone at all.
    (C) Sally's friends do not call her.
    (D) Sally does not have any friends.

12. (A) He celebrated his eighteenth birthday.
    (B) Every eighteen-year-old man is eligible for the army.
    (C) He had a cold on his birthday.
    (D) Drafts cause colds.

13. (A) Anne can drive to Boston with Larry.
    (B) Larry's car is twice as fast as Anne's.
    (C) Larry's car is half as fast as Anne's.
    (D) Anne can drive to Boston in three hours if Larry can.

14. (A) The box is empty.
    (B) The suitcase is larger.
    (C) The suitcase has a box in it.
    (D) The box is bigger.

15. (A) It is eight-fifty now.
    (B) It is nine o'clock now.
    (C) It is nine-ten now.
    (D) It is ten o'clock now.

16. (A) Paul would like to farm.
    (B) Farming is not interesting to Paul.
    (C) Farming is interesting.
    (D) Paul knows how to farm.

17. (A) Carl would like his wife to stop working and stay at home.
    (B) Carl would like his wife to continue working.
    (C) Carl wants to quit his job.
    (D) Carl wants to stay at home.

18. (A) Edith is not a teacher.
    (B) Edith's teacher is like her mother.
    (C) Edith's mother is a teacher.
    (D) Edith likes her teacher.
19. (A) The bus left at midnight.
    (B) The bus left at two o'clock in the afternoon.
    (C) The bus left at ten o'clock in the morning.
    (D) The bus left at ten o'clock at night.
20. (A) The man is downtown.
    (B) The man is in the country.
    (C) The man is at a park.
    (D) The man is at a shopping center.

Part B

Directions: In Part B you will hear 15 short conversations between two speakers. At the end of each conversation, a third voice will ask a question about what was said. The question will be *spoken* just one time. After you hear a conversation and the question about it, read the four possible answers and decide which would be the best response to the question you have heard. Then, on your answer sheet, find the number of the question and mark your answer.

21. (A) The cablevision is not working.
    (B) All of them but channel seventeen.
    (C) Channel seventeen.
    (D) All of them.
22. (A) Mr. Davis.
    (B) Mr. Davis's secretary.
    (C) Mr. Ward.
    (D) Mr. Thomas.
23. (A) At a bank.
    (B) At a grocery store.
    (C) At a doctor's office.
    (D) At a gas station.

24. (A) The man is too tired to go to the movie.
   (B) The woman wants to go to the movie.
   (C) The man wants to go out to dinner.
   (D) The woman does not want to go to the movie.

25. (A) He will borrow some typing paper from the woman.
   (B) He will lend the woman some typing paper.
   (C) He will type the woman's paper.
   (D) He will buy some typing paper for the woman.

26. (A) $60.
   (B) $100.
   (C) $120.
   (D) $200.

27. (A) Two blocks.
   (B) Three blocks.
   (C) Four blocks.
   (D) Five blocks.

28. (A) The man's father did not go.
   (B) The man thought that the game was excellent.
   (C) They thought that the game was unsatisfactory.
   (D) The man thought that the game was excellent, but his father thought that it was unsatisfactory.

29. (A) In a library.
   (B) In a hotel.
   (C) In a hospital.
   (D) In an elevator.

30. (A) $150.
   (B) $175.
   (C) $200.
   (D) $225.

31. (A) Patient-Doctor.
   (B) Waitress-Customer.
   (C) Wife-Husband.
   (D) Secretary-Boss.

32. (A) That the speakers did not go to the meeting.
    (B) That the woman went to the meeting, but the man did not.
    (C) That the man went to the meeting, but the woman did not.
    (D) That both speakers went to the meeting.

33. (A) By December thirtieth.
    (B) By New Year's.
    (C) By December third.
    (D) By December thirteenth.

34. (A) The operator.
    (B) The person receiving the call.
    (C) The person making the call.
    (D) No one. The call is free.

35. (A) At a hotel.
    (B) At a library.
    (C) At a bank.
    (D) At a restaurant.

Part C

Directions: In this part of the test, you will hear several short talks and conversations. After each talk or conversation, you will be asked some questions. The talks and questions will be *spoken* just one time. They will not be written out for you, so you will have to listen carefully in order to understand and remember what the speaker says.

When you hear a question, read the four possible answers in your test book and decide which one would be the best answer to the question you have heard. Then, on your answer sheet, find the number of the problem and fill in (blacken) the space that corresponds to the letter of the answer you have chosen.

MINI-TALK ONE

36. (A) *Third Voyage* and the *Discovery.*
    (B) *Resolution* and the *Discovery.*
    (C) *Revolution* and the *Third Voyage.*
    (D) *England* and the *Discovery.*

37. (A) Nineteen years old.
    (B) Twenty-two years old.
    (C) Thirty years old.
    (D) Forty years old.

38. (A) Iron nails and tools.
    (B) Taro.
    (C) Clothing.
    (D) Cigarettes.

39. (A) England.
    (B) Polynesia.
    (C) Japan.
    (D) China.

40. (A) They fished and raised crops.
    (B) They cared for the children and raised crops.
    (C) They cared for the children and made clothing.
    (D) They made clothing and raised animals.

MINI-TALK TWO

41. (A) *Center.*
    (B) *Centre.*
    (C) *Centr.*
    (D) *Centere.*

42. (A) A smooth surface.
    (B) An actor.
    (C) An apartment.
    (D) A movie.

43. (A) That British English and American English are the same.

(B) That British English and American English are so different that Americans cannot understand Englishmen when they speak.

(C) That British English and American English have different spelling and vocabulary but the same pronunciation.

(D) That British English and American English have slightly different spelling, vocabulary and pronunciation, but Americans and Englishmen still understand each other.

MINI-TALK THREE

44. (A) $1.
(B) $3.
(C) $4.
(D) $5.

45. (A) Jones Jewelry Store.
(B) The Chalet Restaurant.
(C) The Union of City Employees.
(D) Citizen's Bank.

46. (A) Red Sox.
(B) White Sox.
(C) Tigers.
(D) Pirates.

MINI-TALK FOUR

47. (A) Ten o'clock.
(B) One o'clock.
(C) One-thirty.
(D) Two o'clock.

48. (A) Hot.
(B) Warm.
(C) Cool.
(D) Cold.

49. (A) 10 degrees.
    (B) 24 degrees.
    (C) 30 degrees.
    (D) 33 degrees.

50. (A) Tuesday.
    (B) Wednesday.
    (C) Thursday.
    (D) Saturday.

STOP. IF YOU HAVE FINISHED BEFORE TIME IS CALLED, CHECK YOUR WORK ON THIS SECTION ONLY. DO NOT WORK ON ANY OTHER SECTION OF THE TEST.

SECTION II: STRUCTURE AND WRITTEN EXPRESSION

40 QUESTIONS
25 MINUTES

Part A

Directions: In Part A each problem consists of an incomplete sentence. Four words or phrases, each marked (A), (B), (C), (D), are given beneath the sentence. You are to choose the *one* word or phrase that best completes the sentence. Then, on your answer sheet, find the number of the problem and mark your answer.

1. When a body enters the earth's atmosphere, it travels _____.
   - (A) very rapidly
   - (B) in a rapid manner
   - (C) fastly
   - (D) with great speed

2. Put plants _____ a window so that they will get enough light.
   - (A) near to
   - (B) near of
   - (C) next to
   - (D) nearly

3. Employers often require that candidates have not only a degree in engineering _____.
   - (A) but two years experience
   - (B) also two years experience
   - (C) but also two years experience
   - (D) but more two years experience

4. Richard Nixon had been a lawyer and _____ before he entered politics.
   - (A) served in the Navy as an officer
   - (B) an officer in the Navy
   - (C) the Navy had him as an officer
   - (D) did service in the Navy as an officer

5. If one of the participants in a conversation wonders
_____ no real communication has taken place.
   - (A) what said the other person
   - (B) what the other person said
   - (C) what did the other person say
   - (D) what was the other person saying

6. The salary of a bus driver is much higher _____.
   - (A) in comparison with the salary of a teacher
   - (B) than a teacher
   - (C) than that of a teacher
   - (D) to compare as a teacher

7. Professional people appreciate _____ when it is
necessary to cancel an appointment.
   - (A) you to call them
   - (B) that you would call them
   - (C) your calling them
   - (D) that you are calling them

8. The assignment for Monday is to write a _____
about your hometown.
   - (A) five-hundred-word composition
   - (B) five-hundred words composition
   - (C) five-hundreds-words composition
   - (D) five-hundreds-word composition

9. Farmers look forward to _____ every summer.
   - (A) participating in the county fairs
   - (B) participate in the county fairs
   - (C) be participating in the county fairs
   - (D) have participated in the county fairs

10. A computer is usually chosen because of its sim-
plicity of operation and ease of maintenance
_____ its capacity to store information.
   - (A) the same as
   - (B) the same
   - (C) as well as
   - (D) as well

11. Many embarrassing situations occur _____ a misunderstanding.
    - (A) for
    - (B) of
    - (C) because of
    - (D) because

12. Neptune is an extremely cold planet, and _____.
    - (A) so does Uranus
    - (B) so has Uranus
    - (C) so is Uranus
    - (D) Uranus so

13. _____ that gold was discovered at Sutter's Mill, and that the California Gold Rush began.
    - (A) Because in 1848
    - (B) That in 1848
    - (C) In 1848 that it was
    - (D) It was in 1848

14. The crime rate has continued to rise in American cities despite efforts on the part of both government and private citizens to curb _____.
    - (A) them
    - (B) him
    - (C) its
    - (D) it

15. Frost occurs in valleys and on low grounds _____ on adjacent hills.
    - (A) more frequently as
    - (B) as frequently than
    - (C) more frequently than
    - (D) frequently than

Part B

Directions: Each question in Part B consists of a sentence in which four words or phrases are underlined. The four underlined parts of the sentence are marked (A), (B), (C), (D). You are to identify the *one* underlined word or phrase that would *not be accepted* in standard written

English. Then, on your answer sheet, find the number of
the question and mark your answer.

16. The statement <u>will be spoken</u> just one time; there-
                    (A)

   fore, you must listen <u>very careful</u> in order
                          (B)

   <u>to understand</u> <u>what</u> the speaker has said.
       (C)   (D)

17. <u>Every</u> man and woman <u>should vote</u> <u>for</u> the candi-
    (A)   (B)   (C)

   date of <u>their choice</u>.
           (D)

18. In the <u>relatively</u> short history of industrial
           (A)

   <u>developing</u> <u>in the United States</u>, New York City
     (B)   (C)

   <u>has played</u> a vital role.
      (D)

19. As the demand increases, manufacturers who
   <u>previously</u> produced only a large, luxury
     (A)

   car <u>is compelled</u> <u>to make</u> <u>a smaller model</u> in
        (B)   (C)   (D)

   order to compete in the market.

20. For the first time in the history of the country the
   person <u>which</u> <u>was recommended</u> by the presi-
          (A)   (B)

   dent <u>to replace</u> a <u>retiring</u> justice on the Su-
        (C)   (D)

   preme Court is a woman.

21. A prism is used <u>to refract</u> white light <u>so</u> <u>it</u> spreads
                    (A)   (B) (C)

   out in a continuous spectrum <u>of colors</u>.
                                 (D)

22. <u>Despite of</u> rain or snow <u>there are</u> always more
    $\quad$(A)$\qquad\qquad\qquad$(B)

    <u>than</u> fifty thousand fans <u>at</u> the OSU football
    $\quad$(C)$\qquad\qquad\qquad\qquad$(D)

    games.

23. The prices of homes <u>are</u> <u>as</u> high that <u>most</u> people
    $\qquad\qquad\qquad$(A)$\;$(B)$\qquad\qquad$(C)

    cannot afford to buy <u>them</u>.
    $\qquad\qquad\qquad\qquad$(D)

24. To see the Statue of Liberty and <u>taking</u> pictures
    $\qquad\qquad\qquad\qquad\qquad\qquad$(A)

    <u>from</u> the top of the Empire State Building <u>are</u>
    $\;$(B)$\qquad\qquad\qquad\qquad\qquad\qquad\qquad$(C)

    two reasons <u>for visiting</u> New York City.
    $\qquad\qquad\;$(D)

25. There <u>are</u> twenty species of wild roses in North
    $\qquad\;$(A)

    America, all of which <u>have</u> prickly stems, pin-
    $\qquad\qquad\qquad\;$(B)

    nate leaves, and large flowers <u>which</u> usually
    $\qquad\qquad\qquad\qquad\qquad\;$(C)

    smell <u>sweetly</u>.
    $\qquad$(D)

26. <u>Having chose</u> the topics for <u>their</u> essays, the stu-
    $\quad$(A)$\qquad\qquad\qquad$(B)

    dents <u>were</u> instructed to make <u>either</u> a prelim-
    $\qquad$(C)$\qquad\qquad\qquad$(D)

    inary outline or a rough draft.

27. <u>Factoring</u> is the process of <u>finding</u> two or more
    $\;$(A)$\qquad\qquad\qquad$(B)

    expressions <u>whose</u> product is <u>equal as</u> a given
    $\qquad\qquad$(C)$\qquad\qquad$(D)

    expression.

28. If Grandma Moses <u>having</u> been able to continue
    $\qquad\qquad\qquad$(A)

    <u>farming</u> she may never have <u>begun</u> <u>to paint</u>.
    $\;$(B)$\qquad\qquad\qquad\qquad$(C)$\quad$(D)

29. Since infection <u>can cause</u> both fever <u>as well as</u>
                    (A)   (B)
    pain, it is a good idea <u>to check</u> <u>his</u> temperature.
                            (C)   (D)

30. <u>In response to</u> <u>question thirteen</u>, I enjoy <u>modern</u> art,
       (A)   (B)   (C)
    classical music, and <u>to read</u>.
                         (D)

31. They asked us, Henry and I, whether we <u>thought</u>
                            (A)   (B)
    that the statistics <u>had been presented</u> <u>fairly</u> and
                        (C)   (D)
    accurately.

32. <u>In purchasing</u> a <u>winter coat</u>, it is <u>very</u> important
       (A)   (B)   (C)
    <u>for trying</u> it on with heavy clothing underneath.
       (D)

33. <u>What happened</u> in New York <u>were</u> a reaction from
       (A)   (B)
    city workers, <u>including</u> firemen and policemen
                    (C)
    who had been laid off from <u>their jobs</u>.
                               (D)

34. I sometimes wish that my university <u>is</u> <u>as large as</u>
                                        (A)   (B)
    State University because our facilities are
    <u>more</u> limited <u>than</u> theirs.
     (C)   (D)

35. Some executives insist <u>that</u> the secretary <u>is</u> respon-
                           (A)   (B)
    sible for <u>writing</u> all reports <u>as well as</u> for bal-
               (C)   (D)
    ancing the books.

36. Although a doctor may be able <u>to diagnose</u> a prob-
                                    (A)
    lem <u>perfect</u>, he still may not <u>be able to</u> find a
        (B)   (C)
    drug <u>to which</u> the patient responds.
         (D)

37. Although the Red Cross <u>accepts</u> blood from most
                            (A)
    donors, the nurses will not <u>leave</u> you <u>give</u> blood
                                (B)   (C)
    if you have just <u>had</u> a cold.
                     (D)

38. A turtle differs <u>from</u> all <u>other</u> reptiles in that it has
                     (A)   (B)
    its body encased in a protective shell of <u>their</u>
                                              (C)
    <u>own</u>.
    (D)

39. Benjamin Franklin <u>was</u> the editor of <u>the largest</u>
                       (A)   (B)
    newspaper in the colonies, a diplomatic rep-
    resentative to France and later to England, and
    <u>he invented</u> <u>many</u> useful devices.
     (C)   (D)

40. Professor Baker told her class that a good way
    <u>to improve</u> listening comprehension skills <u>is</u>
     (A)   (B)
    <u>to watch</u> television, <u>especially</u> news programs
     (C)   (D)
    and documentaries.

STOP. IF YOU HAVE FINISHED BEFORE TIME IS CALLED, CHECK YOUR
WORK ON THIS SECTION ONLY. DO NOT WORK ON ANY OTHER SECTION
OF THE TEST.

SECTION III: READING COMPREHENSION
AND VOCABULARY

60 QUESTIONS
55 MINUTES

Part A

Directions: In each sentence of Part A, a word or phrase is underlined. Below each sentence are four other words or phrases. You are to choose the one word or phrase which would *best keep the meaning* of the original sentence if it were substituted for the underlined word.

1. Unorganized guessing will probably not raise a test score as significantly as choosing one letter as a "guess answer" for the entire examination.
   - (A) Cryptic
   - (B) Haphazard
   - (C) Economical
   - (D) Subsequent

2. The thief was apprehended, but his accomplice had disappeared.
   - (A) people who saw him
   - (B) guns and knives
   - (C) person who helped him
   - (D) stolen goods

3. Electrical energy may be divided into two components specified as positive and negative.
   - (A) confused
   - (B) designated
   - (C) accumulated
   - (D) separated

4. Owners should be sure that their insurance will replace all of their merchandise.
   - (A) Proprietors
   - (B) Tutors
   - (C) Benefactors
   - (D) Debtors

5. The Mona Lisa is the portrait of a woman with a very enticing smile.
   - (A) oblivious
   - (B) luminous
   - (C) alluring
   - (D) elusive

6. When one is unfamiliar with the customs, it is easy to make a blunder.
   - (A) a commitment
   - (B) a mistake
   - (C) an enemy
   - (D) an injury

7. A <u>vacant</u> apartment in New York City is very difficult to find.
   - (A) good
   - (B) large
   - (C) empty
   - (D) clean

8. Astronomy provides the knowledge necessary for <u>correct</u> time-keeping, navigation, surveying, and map making.
   - (A) meticulous
   - (B) incessant
   - (C) accurate
   - (D) ancient

9. In several states, the people may recommend a law to the legislature by signing a <u>request</u>.
   - (A) compromise
   - (B) manuscript
   - (C) budget
   - (D) petition

10. In a <u>search</u> to further his knowledge of the unknown, man has explored the earth, the sea, and now, outer space.
    - (A) quest
    - (B) colloquy
    - (C) fantasy
    - (D) documentary

11. Because tornados are more <u>prevalent</u> in the middle states, the area from Minnesota to Texas is called Tornado Alley.
    - (A) severe
    - (B) widespread
    - (C) short-lived
    - (D) feared

12. One must <u>live in</u> the United States five years in order to apply for citizenship.
    - (A) reside in
    - (B) accommodate to
    - (C) invade
    - (D) abandon

13. Reagan seemed <u>sure</u> that he would win the election.
    - (A) eager
    - (B) hopeful
    - (C) confident
    - (D) resigned

14. Even though the critics are not enthusiastic, some of the plays off Broadway are <u>very funny</u>.
    - (A) incongruous
    - (B) anomalous
    - (C) illustrious
    - (D) hilarious

15. Ethnocentrism prevents us from <u>putting up with</u> all of the customs we encounter in another culture.
    - (A) experiencing
    - (B) adopting
    - (C) comprehending
    - (D) tolerating

16. For your safety and the safety of others, always <u>pay attention to</u> traffic signals.

(A) overlook   (C) glance at

(B) heed   (D) repair

17. Neon is an element which does not combine readily with any other element; because of this property, it is called an <u>inactive</u> element.

(A) inert   (C) explicit

(B) adjacent   (D) obsolete

18. Attending a church, temple, or mosque is one way to make <u>agreeable</u> friends.

(A) enduring   (C) elderly

(B) congenial   (D) numerous

19. Because the Amtrak system is so old, the trains always start <u>suddenly</u>.

(A) with ease   (C) with a jerk

(B) with a thump   (D) with effort

20. In order to enjoy fine wine, one should <u>drink</u> it slowly, a little at a time.

(A) stir it   (C) spill it

(B) sniff it   (D) sip it

21. Unless the <u>agreement</u> contains a provision for a United Nations peace-keeping force to patrol the borders, the General Assembly is not likely to ratify it.

(A) proposal   (C) concord

(B) document   (D) release

22. When Joan of Arc described her vision, her voice did not <u>hesitate</u>.

(A) amplify   (C) dissolve

(B) falter   (D) mumble

23. The cost of living in the United States has risen at a rate of 6 percent per year during the last <u>ten-year period</u>.

(A) tenth   (C) decade

(B) century   (D) quarter

24. Primary education in the U.S. is <u>compulsory</u>.
    (A) free of charge   (C) excellent
    (B) required   (D) easy

25. During the Great Depression, there were many <u>wanderers</u> who traveled on the railroads and camped along the tracks.
    (A) vagabonds   (C) zealots
    (B) tyros   (D) veterans

26. The Civil War in 1863 <u>cut</u> the United States in two nations—a southern Confederacy and a northern Union.
    (A) severed   (C) integrated
    (B) acknowledged   (D) alienated

27. The National Institute of Mental Health is conducting <u>far-reaching</u> research to determine the psychological effects of using drugs.
    (A) extensive   (C) refined
    (B) prevalent   (D) tentative

28. In American football, the coach may <u>shout</u> to the captain to call time out.
    (A) yelp   (C) bellow
    (B) growl   (D) flounder

29. A monument was erected in memory of those who died in the <u>disaster</u> at Johnstown, Pennsylvania.
    (A) prison   (C) cataclysm
    (B) skirmish   (D) frontier

30. Martin Luther King <u>detested</u> injustice.
    (A) recognized   (C) suffered
    (B) confronted   (D) abhorred

Part B

Directions: In Part B, you will be given a variety of reading material (single sentences, paragraphs, advertisements, and the like) followed by questions about the meaning of the material. You are to choose the *one* best answer, (A), (B), (C), or (D), to each question. Then, on your answer sheet, find the number of the problem and mark your answer. Answer all questions following a passage on the basis of what is *stated* or *implied* in that passage.

Questions 31–35 refer to the following passage:

The general principles of dynamics are rules which demonstrate a relationship between the motions of bodies and the forces which produce those motions. Based in large part on the work of his predecessors, Sir Isaac Newton deduced three laws of dynamics which he published in 1687 in his famous *Principia*.

Prior to Newton, Aristotle had established that the natural state of a body was a state of rest, and that unless a force acted upon it to maintain motion, a moving body would come to rest. Galileo had succeeded in correctly describing the behavior of falling objects and in recording that no force was required to maintain a body in motion. He noted that the effect of force was to change motion. Huygens recognized that a change in the direction of motion involved acceleration, just as did a change in speed, and further, that the action of a force was required. Kepler deduced the laws describing the motion of planets around the sun. It was primarily from Galileo and Kepler that Newton borrowed.

31. Which of the following scientists established that the natural state of a body was a state of rest?
    (A) Galileo   (C) Aristotle
    (B) Kepler   (D) Newton

32. Huygens stated that acceleration was required
    (A) for either a change in direction or a change in speed
    (B) only for a change in speed
    (C) only for a change in direction
    (D) neither for a change in direction nor for a change in speed

33. The first scientist to correctly describe the behavior of falling objects was
(A) Aristotle
(C) Kepler
(B) Newton
(D) Galileo

34. According to this passage, Newton based his laws primarily upon the work of
(A) Galileo and Copernicus
(B) Ptolemy and Copernicus
(C) Huygens and Kepler
(D) Galileo and Kepler

35. What is the main purpose of this passage?
(A) To demonstrate the development of Newton's laws
(B) To establish Newton as the authority in the field of physics
(C) To discredit Newton's laws of motion
(D) To describe the motion of planets around the sun

Questions 36–39 refer to the following course description:

---

206. American English Phonetics. Fall. 5 hours. Three lectures, two laboratory periods. *Prerequisite:* English 205, Linguistics 210 or equivalent. A study of American English pronunciation, designed for advanced international students. Professor Ayers.

---

36. From this course description, we know that the class meets
(A) two hours a day
(B) three hours a week
(C) five hours a day
(D) five hours a week

37. In order to take American English Phonetics it is necessary to
- (A) take English 206 first
- (B) know the material from English 205 or Linguistics 210
- (C) have permission from Professors Ayers
- (D) pass an examination

38. Students who take this course should expect to
- (A) study British English
- (B) be taught by international students
- (C) study English 205 and Linguistics 210 at the same time
- (D) use a language laboratory twice a week

39. This course will probably be offered from
- (A) January to March
- (B) April to June
- (C) July to August
- (D) September to December

Questions 40–42 refer to the following sentence:

Horace Mann, the first secretary of the state board of education in Massachusetts, exercised an enormous influence during the critical period of reconstruction which brought into existence the American graded elementary school as a substitute for the older district school system.

40. Horace Mann's influence on American education was
- (A) very great
- (B) small, but important
- (C) misunderstood
- (D) not accepted

41. Horace Mann advocated
- (A) the state board school system
- (B) the district school system
- (C) the substitute school system
- (D) the graded school system

42. The graded elementary school
    - (A) replaced the district school system
    - (B) was used only in Massachusetts
    - (C) was rejected by the secretary of the state board of education
    - (D) was the first school system established in America

Questions 43–45 refer to the following passage:

The population of the world has increased more in modern times than in all other ages of history combined. World population totaled about 500 million in 1650. It doubled in the period from 1650–1850. Today the population is more than three billion. Estimates based on research by the United Nations indicate that it will more than double in the next twenty-five years, reaching seven billion by the year 2000.

43. By 1850, approximately what was the world population?
    - (A) 500 million
    - (B) one billion
    - (C) three billion
    - (D) seven billion

44. World population doubled in the years between
    - (A) 500–1650
    - (B) 1650–1850
    - (C) 1650–today
    - (D) 1850–2000

45. According to this passage, by the year 2000 the earth's population should exceed the present figure by
    - (A) 500 million
    - (B) three billion
    - (C) four billion
    - (D) seven billion

Questions 46–48 refer to the following passage:

In the undergraduate schools and colleges, a student will be classified according to the number of academic quarter hours that he or she has completed with an average grade of 2.0 or better.

Classification	Hours Completed
Freshman	Less than 45 hours
Sophomore	At least 45 hours
Junior	At least 90 hours
Senior	At least 140 hours

46. How would a student with 45 credit hours be classified?
    - (A) Freshman
    - (B) Sophomore
    - (C) Junior
    - (D) Senior

47. How would a student with 96 credit hours be classified?
    - (A) Freshman
    - (B) Sophomore
    - (C) Junior
    - (D) Senior

48. Which of the following would most likely represent the number of credit hours earned by a senior?
    - (A) 100
    - (B) 140
    - (C) 139
    - (D) 90

Questions 49–51 refer to the following passage:

Organic architecture, that is, natural architecture, may be varied in concept and form, but it is always faithful to principle. Organic architecture rejects rules imposed by individual preference or mere aesthetics in order to remain true to the nature of the site, the materials, the purpose of the structure, and the people who will ultimately use it. If this natural principle is upheld, then a bank cannot be built to look like a Greek temple. Form does not follow function; form is inseparable from function.

49. Another name for organic architecture is
    - (A) natural architecture
    - (B) aesthetic architecture
    - (C) principle architecture
    - (D) varied architecture

50. In organic architecture
    (A) form follows function
    (B) function follows form
    (C) function is not important to form
    (D) form and function are one

51. A good example of organic architecture is a
    (A) bank that is built to look like a Greek temple
    (B) bank built so that the location is unimportant to the structure
    (C) bank that is built to conform to the natural surroundings
    (D) bank that is built to be beautiful rather than functional

Questions 52–55 refer to the following passage:

The earliest authentic works on European alchemy are those of the English monk Roger Bacon and the German philosopher St. Albertus Magnus. In their treatises they maintained that gold was the perfect metal and that inferior metals such as lead and mercury were removed by various degrees of imperfection from gold. They further asserted that these base metals could be transmuted to gold by blending them with a substance even more perfect than gold. This elusive substance was referred to as the "philosopher's stone."

52. Roger Bacon and St. Albertus Magnus had the same
    (A) nationality   (C) profession
    (B) premise   (D) education

53. It is probable that Roger Bacon's work
    (A) was not genuine
    (B) disproved that of St. Albertus Magnus
    (C) was written after St. Albertus Magnus
    (D) contained references to the conversion of base metals to gold

54. According to the alchemists, the difference between base metals and gold was one of
    (A) perfection   (C) temperature
    (B) chemical content   (D) weight

55. The "philosopher's stone" was
    (A) lead which was mixed with gold
    (B) an element which was never found
    (C) another name for alchemy
    (D) a base metal

Questions 56–60. For each of these questions, choose the answer that is closest in meaning to the original sentence. Note that several of the choices may be factually correct, but you should choose the one that is the closest restatement of the given sentence.

56. Despite a large advertising campaign, the new business could not compete with the established firms.
    (A) Advertising helped the new business to compete with the established firms.
    (B) The established firms advertised so that the new business would not be able to compete with them.
    (C) Even though the new business advertised, they could not compete with the established firms.
    (D) Because the advertising campaign was new, the business could not compete with the established firms.

57. It is necessary to have a doctor's prescription in order to buy most medicines in the United States.
    (A) In the United States, medicine must be bought with prescriptions instead of money.
    (B) In most of the states, doctors give prescriptions for medicine.
    (C) Most medicine cannot be bought without a prescription in the United States.
    (D) In the United States, most doctors give prescriptions for medicine.

58. Taking notes, even incomplete ones, is usually more efficient than relying on one's memory.
    (A) Because notes are usually incomplete, it is more efficient to rely on one's memory.
    (B) It is usually more efficient to take incomplete notes than to rely on one's memory.
    (C) Taking incomplete notes is usually less efficient than relying on one's memory.
    (D) One's memory is usually more efficient than incomplete notes.

59. The National Weather Service issued a tornado warning just minutes before a funnel cloud was sighted in the area.
    (A) After sighting a funnel cloud, the National Weather Service issued a tornado warning.
    (B) After the National Weather Service issued a tornado warning, a funnel cloud was sighted in the area.
    (C) When they saw a funnel cloud at the National Weather Service, they issued a tornado warning.
    (D) A tornado warning was issued by the National Weather Service after a funnel cloud was sighted in the area.

60. The interest rate on a minimum balance savings account is a little higher than the interest rate on a regular savings account.
    (A) A regular savings account draws higher interest than an account which has a minimum balance.
    (B) The interest rate is lower for a minimum balance savings account than for a regular account.
    (C) A savings account in which a minimum balance is maintained draws higher interest than a regular savings account.
    (D) A minimum interest rate, lower than a regular rate, is drawn on a balanced savings account.

STOP. IF YOU HAVE FINISHED BEFORE TIME IS CALLED, CHECK YOUR WORK ON THIS SECTION ONLY. DO NOT WORK ON ANY OTHER SECTION OF THE TEST.

Answer Key—Model Test 2

Section I: Listening Comprehension

1. (D)	11. (A)	21. (C)	31. (B)	41. (B)
2. (A)	12. (B)	22. (C)	32. (A)	42. (C)
3. (B)	13. (B)	23. (D)	33. (D)	43. (D)
4. (A)	14. (D)	24. (D)	34. (B)	44. (C)
5. (D)	15. (C)	25. (D)	35. (A)	45. (D)
6. (B)	16. (B)	26. (A)	36. (B)	46. (A)
7. (C)	17. (A)	27. (D)	37. (D)	47. (B)
8. (C)	18. (C)	28. (C)	38. (A)	48. (D)
9. (C)	19. (D)	29. (C)	39. (B)	49. (A)
10. (C)	20. (D)	30. (B)	40. (C)	50. (D)

Section II: Structure and Written Expression

1. (A)	9. (A)	17. (D)	25. (D)	33. (B)
2. (B)	10. (C)	18. (B)	26. (A)	34. (A)
3. (C)	11. (C)	19. (B)	27. (D)	35. (B)
4. (B)	12. (C)	20. (A)	28. (A)	36. (B)
5. (B)	13. (D)	21. (B)	29. (B)	37. (B)
6. (C)	14. (D)	22. (A)	30. (D)	38. (C)
7. (C)	15. (C)	23. (B)	31. (A)	39. (C)
8. (A)	16. (B)	24. (A)	32. (D)	40. (B)

Section III: Reading Comprehension and Vocabulary

1. (B)	13. (C)	25. (A)	37. (B)	49. (A)
2. (C)	14. (D)	26. (A)	38. (D)	50. (D)
3. (B)	15. (D)	27. (A)	39. (D)	51. (C)
4. (A)	16. (B)	28. (C)	40. (A)	52. (B)
5. (C)	17. (A)	29. (C)	41. (D)	53. (D)
6. (B)	18. (B)	30. (D)	42. (A)	54. (A)
7. (C)	19. (C)	31. (C)	43. (B)	55. (B)
8. (C)	20. (D)	32. (A)	44. (B)	56. (C)
9. (D)	21. (C)	33. (D)	45. (C)	57. (C)
10. (A)	22. (B)	34. (D)	46. (B)	58. (B)
11. (B)	23. (C)	35. (A)	47. (C)	59. (B)
12. (A)	24. (B)	36. (D)	48. (B)	60. (C)

Transcript for the Listening Comprehension Test—Model Test 2

In this section of the test, you will have an opportunity to demonstrate your ability to understand spoken English. It is in three parts, and there are special directions for each part. [For the directions to each part, see the corresponding portion in the test. The listening comprehension section is on the cassette included with this test book.]

Part A

Directions: For the directions to this part, see page 155.

(*Note:* The reader should say the question number preceding each test question. For example, the reader should say, "Question number one. She thought that Bob was single . . .")

1. She thought that Bob was single because he wasn't wearing a ring, but he was married.

(*Note:* There should be a 15-second pause after each test question in this section.)

2. Mrs. Black told her son to take an umbrella with him.
3. You'll have to leave at seven-thirty in order to get to the play by eight-thirty.
4. Bill wants to trade his big car for a smaller model.
5. Ms. Kent is in court right now, but if you leave your number, I'll have her return your call.
6. If Jim had been paying attention, he would have heard the question.
7. When I called the dormitory to see if Joe was there, the head resident said that he was in the hospital.

8. We had only expected twenty people to register for the course, but twice as many showed up on the first day of classes.

9. It would have been a perfect paper except for one misspelled word.

10. The concert was supposed to begin at eight o'clock, but it was delayed fifteen minutes.

11. Sally likes nothing better than to talk on the telephone with her friends.

12. Every American man is eligible for the draft on his eighteenth birthday.

13. If Anne can drive to Boston in six hours, Larry should be able to make it in three hours in his car.

14. This box will hold more than that suitcase.

15. Hurry up. The second movie started at nine o'clock, and we're already ten minutes late.

16. Paul isn't interested in farming.

17. Carl wants his wife to quit her job and stay home with the children.

18. Edith is a teacher like her mother.

19. Dick got to the bus station at midnight, missing his bus by two hours.

20. I'd rather get my groceries here than downtown because there's more parking space; besides, there's a big department store near in case I need anything else.

Part B

Directions: For the directions to this part, see page 158.

(*Note:* In this section, three readers are required: one man, one woman, and one narrator—either man or woman. The narrator reads the question number and the question following the dialogue.)

21. *Woman:*   There's something wrong with the TV. Only channel seventeen has a good picture.

   Man: Maybe the cablevision isn't working.

   Third Voice: Which channel has a good picture?

(*Note:* There should be a 15-second pause after each test question in this section.)

22. *Man:*   Hello. I'd like to speak with Mr. Davis, please. This is Thomas Ward with the Office of Immigrations.

   Woman: I'm sorry, Mr. Ward. Mr. Davis is in conference now.

   Third Voice: Who works for the Immigrations Office?

23. *Woman:*   Fill it up with regular and check the oil, please.

   Man: Right away, Miss.

   Third Voice: Where did this conversation most probably take place?

24. *Man:*   Let's go to the movies after dinner.

   Woman: Well, I'll go if you really want to, but I'm a little bit tired.

   Third Voice: What conclusion does the woman want us to make from her statement?

25. *Woman:*   I'm out of typing paper. Will you lend me some?

   Man: I don't have any either, but I'll be glad to get you some when I go to the bookstore.

   Third Voice: What is the man going to do?

26. *Woman:*   I like these chairs. How much are they?

   Man: They are sixty dollars each or one hundred dollars for the pair.

   Third Voice: How much does one chair cost?

27. *Man:*   Excuse me. Could you please tell me how to get to the University City Bank?

	Woman:	Sure. Go straight for two blocks, then turn left and walk three more blocks until you get to the drug store. It's right across the street.
	Third Voice:	How far must the man walk to get to the bank?
28.	Woman:	How did you and your dad like the football game yesterday?
	Man:	Oh. They played so poorly that we left at the half-time.
	Third Voice:	How did the man and his father feel about the football game?
29.	Man:	Excuse me, nurse. I'm looking for the emergency room. I thought that it was on the first floor.
	Woman:	It is. This is the basement. Take the elevator one flight up and turn left.
	Third Voice:	Where did this conversation most probably take place?
30.	Man:	How much is the rent?
	Woman:	It's a hundred and fifty dollars a month unfurnished or two hundred dollars a month furnished. Utilities are twenty-five dollars extra.
	Third Voice:	How much will it cost the man to rent an unfurnished apartment, including utilities?
31.	Woman:	Would you like to see a menu?
	Man:	No, thank you. I already know what I want to order.
	Third Voice:	What is the probable relationship between the two speakers?
32.	Woman:	Didn't you go to the meeting last night either?
	Man:	No. I had a slight headache.
	Third Voice:	What do we understand from this conversation?

33. *Woman:* Your library books are due on December thirteenth. If you haven't finished using them by then, you may renew them once.

    Man: Thank you very much. I only need them for a few days.

    Third Voice: When must the man return his books to the library?

34. *Man:* Operator, I want to place a long distance call collect to Columbus, Ohio. The area code is six-one-four and the number is four-two-nine, seven-five-eight-three.

    Woman: Thank you. I'll ring it for you.

    Third Voice: Who will pay for the call?

35. *Man:* I'd like to check in, please. I didn't make a reservation.

    Woman: That's not necessary, sir. Just sign the register.

    Third Voice: Where did this conversation most probably take place?

Part C

Directions: For the directions to this part, see page 160.

MINI-TALK ONE

Let's begin with a brief review of yesterday's lecture before we continue. As you will recall, Captain James Cook, at the age of forty, was commissioned by England to explore the Pacific Ocean.

On his third exploratory voyage, as captain in charge of two ships, the *Resolution* and the *Discovery*, he came upon a group of uncharted islands which he named the Sandwich Islands as a tribute to his good friend, the Earl of Sandwich. Today the islands are known as the Hawaiian Islands.

When Cook sailed into a protected bay of one of the larger islands, the natives greeted him with curiosity and respect. Some historians contend that the islanders welcomed him, believing that he was the god Launo, protector of peace and agriculture.

The islanders were short, strong people, with a very well-organized social system. The men fished and raised crops including taro, coconuts, sweet potatoes, and sugar cane. The women cared for the children and made clothing that consisted of loin cloths for the men and short skirts for the women.

Poi was the staple food, made from taro root. It has been suggested that the seeds of taro and other crops had been brought from Polynesia centuries before.

The natives were especially eager to exchange food and supplies for iron nails and tools, and Captain Cook was easily able to restock his ship before he sailed.

Because of a severe storm in which the *Resolution* was damaged, it was necessary to return to Hawaii. Now sure that Cook and his crew were men and not gods, the natives welcomed them less hospitably. Besides, diseases brought by the English had reached epidemic proportions. When a small boat was stolen from the *Discovery*, Cook demanded that the king be taken as a hostage until the boat was returned.

In the fighting that followed, Cook and four other crewmen were killed. Within a week the ship had been repaired, and on February 22, 1779, both ships departed again.

Today we will begin a discussion of the kingdom of Hawaii in the nineteenth century and of its eventual annexation to the United States.

36. According to the lecturer, what were the two ships commanded by Captain Cook?

(*Note:* There should be a 15-second pause after each test question in this section.)

37. How old was Captain Cook when he was commissioned to explore the Pacific Ocean?

38. What did Captain Cook trade in exchange for food and supplies?

39. It was believed that the seeds and plants on the islands had originally come from where?

40. What did the native women do?

MINI-TALK TWO

John: British English and American English are really about the same, aren't they?

Mary: I don't think so. It seems to me that some of the spellings are different.

Baker: You're right, Mary. Words like *theater* and *center* end in *r-e* in England instead of in *e-r* like we spell them. Can you think of any more examples?

Mary: The word *color*?

Baker: Good. In fact, many words which end in *o-r* in American English are spelled *o-u-r* in British English.

John: I'm still not convinced. I mean, if someone comes here from England, we can all understand what he's saying. The spelling doesn't really matter that much.

Baker: Okay. Are we just talking about spelling? Or are there some differences in pronunciation and meaning too?

Mary: Professor Baker?

Baker: Yes.

Mary: I remember seeing an English movie where the actors kept calling their apartment a *flat*. Half of the movie was over before I realized what they were talking about.

John: So there are slight differences in spelling and some vocabulary.

Mary: And pronunciation, too. You aren't going to tell me that you sound like Richard Burton.

John: Richard Burton isn't English. He's Welsh.

Mary: Okay. Anyway, the pronunciation is different.

Baker: I think that what we are really disagreeing about is the extent of the difference. We all agree that British English and American English are different. Right?

Mary: Yes.

John: Sure.

Baker: But not so different that it prevents us from understanding each other.

John: That's what I mean.

Mary: That's what I mean, too.

41. According to this class discussion, how is the word *center* spelled in British English?

42. What does the word *flat* mean in British English?

43. On what did the class agree?

MINI-TALK THREE

Good afternoon. This is Gene Edwards with the local news brought to you by Citizen's Bank.

In the headlines today: new traffic rates, a fire at a downtown restaurant, a welcome end to the city workers' strike, and a final score on the Little League baseball championship.

Remember that today new overtime parking rates went into effect all over the city. Yellow tickets for parking overtime at a downtown meter will now cost two dollars if paid within twenty-four hours. The old rate was one dollar. The cost goes up from three dollars to five dollars if paid after the twenty-four-hour period. Red tickets will now cost four dollars, up a dollar from the old three-dollar rate.

An early morning fire that started in the kitchen of the Chalet Restaurant, 1400 Market Street, caused extensive damage to the restaurant and to the adjoining Jones Jewelry Store.

Both the restaurant and the jewelry store suffered smoke and water damage. Fire Chief Bill Howard estimated the loss in excess of one hundred thousand dollars on the buildings alone. Owners had not estimated the loss of contents by news time.

Roofs on several nearby buildings were ignited, but quickly extinguished. The cause of the fire is not known.

Mayor Carl Rogers said that a tentative agreement had been reached last night with city workers, ending the strike which had disrupted city services since last Monday.

Rogers said that Union Local one-fifty of City Employees had been granted a contract guaranteeing them a ten-cent-an-hour raise for this year and a twenty-five-cent-an-hour raise for next year.

Members of the Local are expected to report back to their jobs tomorrow morning.

Little League baseball Friday night featured games in both the lower and upper divisions. In the lower division, the Pirates lost to the Tigers by only one run. The final score on that game was seven-six.

In the upper division, the Red Sox defeated the White Sox eight to five in a play-off to determine the winner of the city championship.

You are listening to the Voice of Washington State. This is WXYW, the Pacific Ocean station. The news at noon has been brought to you by Citizen's Bank.

44. What will the new overtime parking rate be for a red ticket?

45. What store sponsored the news broadcast?

46. Which team won the Little League city championship?

MINI-TALK FOUR

And now for a look at the weather. Cold and windy with a chance of afternoon snow flurries. Today's high was thirty-three degrees. Partly cloudy and continued cold tonight and tomorrow, with tonight's low near ten degrees and tomorrow's high around twenty-four degrees.

We have a forty percent chance of snow this afternoon, and a twenty percent chance tomorrow. At one o'clock our current temperature is thirty degrees.

On the extended outlook, partly cloudy skies and near-freezing temperatures Tuesday, Wednesday, and Thursday, with little chance of snow until the weekend.

47. What time was this weather forecast reported?

48. What, in general terms, is the weather?

49. According to the weatherman, what will the low temperature be tonight?

50. When is it likely to snow?